6 Am.   Every other Thursday.
Oct 3   Chap 1.

Joshua

MEN *of* CHARACTER

Joshua

Living as a Consistent Role Model

GENE A. GETZ

Foreword by Frank Minirth, M.D.

BROADMAN
& HOLMAN
PUBLISHERS

Nashville, Tennessee

Published by:
Broadman & Holman Publishers
Nashville, Tennessee

Design:
Steven Boyd

4261-63
0-8054-6163-9

Dewey Decimal Classification: 248.842
Subject Heading: Men \ Joshua \ Christian Life
Library of Congress Card Catalog Number: 94-40764

Unless otherwise noted, Scripture quotations are from the New American Standard Bible, © the Lockman Foundation, 1960, 1962, 1963, 1968, 1971, 1972, 1973, 1975, 1977; used by permission. Passages marked NIV are from the Holy Bible, New International Version, copyright © 1973, 1978, 1984 by International Bible Society; and NKJV, the New King James Version, copyright © 1979, 1980, 1982, Thomas Nelson, Inc., Publishers.

Library of Congress Cataloging-in-Publication Data
Getz, Gene A.
    Joshua : living as a consistent role model / Gene Getz.
        p. cm. — (Men of character)
    Rev. ed.
    Includes bibliographical references.
    ISBN 0-8054-6163-9
    1. Joshua (biblical figure).   2. Bible. O. T. Joshua—Criticism, interpretation, etc. I. Title. II. Series: Getz, Gene A. Men of character.
    BS580.J7G47   1995
    222'.2092—dc20
    94-40764
    CIP
            7   8   9   10   04   03   02

This book on Joshua is affectionately dedicated to Virgil Stoneking, a longtime friend. Virgil first introduced me to Chuck Wilson, vice-president Trade Publishing/publisher Broadman & Holman Publishers, which resulted in a wonderful publisher-author relationship. So, thanks, Virgil, for building this unique bridge.

Contents

Foreword

One of the most dynamic and practical ways to learn biblical principles for daily Christian living is to study Old Testament characters. I don't believe anyone does a better job introducing us to these biblical personalities and drawing lessons from their lives than my good friend and pastor Gene Getz.

I've known Gene for many years. In fact, when I first came to Dallas to begin my psychiatric practice, we taught pastoral psychology and counseling together at Dallas Theological Seminary. As a tenured professor and one who "knew the ropes," Gene really helped me to acclimate to the seminary environment. Over the years, I've observed firsthand that Gene Getz practices what he preaches in his personal life, in his marriage and family, and in his professional life.

Later, Gene became pastor to my family—and still is. I've listened to him recount these Old Testament stories from the pulpit. In fact, as I write the foreword to this book on Joshua, Gene is just completing an exciting study on Jacob.

What makes these studies so powerful is Gene's ability to not only unfold the biblical facts about their lives but to explore their unique personalities—their strengths, their weaknesses, their emotional highs and lows, and their spiritual struggles. In short, his biblical insights combined with his psychological wisdom enables Gene to help us understand and learn from these men who lived long ago.

Another unique aspect of these studies is Gene's extraordinary ability to abstract principles that are supracultural and forever relevant. He effectively integrates Old Testament insights with New Testament truths.

This stimulating study of Joshua is a role model for Christian men today. It will enrich the readers' lives by providing real examples and guidance for the choices and challenges of today's world.

Frank Minirth
Founder and Co-CEO
The Minirth Meier New Life Clinics

An Old Testament Warrior

One of the most exciting ways for every twentieth-century man to learn practical lessons for facing today's challenges successfully is to study Old Testament Bible characters. Joshua is one of those. Perhaps more than any other Old Testament person, Joshua exemplifies for every man, particularly, positive ways to live a victorious Christian life. He walks through the battlefields of the Old Testament as a godly man. Though he certainly made mistakes, he lived an exemplary life.

Most of what we learn about Joshua is recorded in the book that bears his name—the sixth book in the Old Testament.[1] And though the *man* Joshua is the focus of our study, most of the lessons that we can learn from his life involve his relationship with others—the children of Israel, the Canaanites, and the unique individuals who were closely identified with him in the conquest of the land.

Doing Battle Against the Forces of Evil

What can a twentieth-century Christian man living in a vastly different culture learn from a man like Joshua? Admittedly, he was definitely a military leader operating in a very primitive environment. His greatest task was to lead the armies of Israel to take possession of the land of Canaan. However, many of the challenges he faced are essentially the same challenges that an American man faces today as he does battle against the forces of evil that are trying to capture his heart and mind.

While facing literal battles, Joshua demonstrates how men today can be "strong in the Lord and in his mighty power" by "clothing themselves" with "the full armor of God" in order to defeat "the powers of this dark world" and "the spiritual forces of evil in the heavenly realms" (Eph. 6:10–12, NIV).

Listening to Our Spiritual Commander-in-chief

As we study the life of this Old Testament warrior, we can learn dynamic lessons for living victoriously. In essence, these lessons come from God Himself, though we will see they are fleshed out in Joshua's experience.

- ➤ God understands our human weaknesses—our fears, our anxieties, our feelings of inadequacy.

- ➤ God promises security and inner peace in the midst of fear and stress.

- ➤ God wants all people to be saved from their sins and He continues to reach out to lost humanity—no matter what their background, their mistakes, their evil deeds, their depth of despair, or their idolatrous and pagan behavior.

- ➤ God honors and responds to faith but He does not expect His children to operate on "blind" faith.

- ➤ God honors those who honor Him.

- ➤ When the family ceases to reflect God's values, it takes only one generation for spiritual degeneration to take place.

- ➤ As twentieth-century Christians, we need "remembrances" lest we forget what God has done for us.

- ➤ God can take even our mistakes and turn them into positive results.

➤ We must take time on a consistent basis to maintain perspective on God's will for our lives.

➤ True love for God is the essence of Christian living.

➤ Doing the will of God involves a personal choice—an act of the will.

These are some of the dynamic and practical lessons you'll learn from Joshua. Welcome to an exciting study.

Chapter 1

Joshua's Basic Training
Read 2 Timothy 2:1–4

*J*oshua was a leader—and so are you! When you became a Christian, you inherited a leadership role. You may not be president of a corporation or the pastor of a church, but you *are* a leader in God's great army of believers. For starters, you're called to model Jesus Christ—and that's leadership. Someone is looking to you—your wife, your children, a friend—and how you function at this level of leadership will determine your advancement.

That Culprit Called "Impatience"

Have you ever become impatient because God's timetable doesn't match yours—especially in giving you a position of respect and recognition? I remember facing that struggle in my own life. Little did I realize *then* how much I had to learn about being a leader. Now, years later, I am more aware of how immature I really was back then. And, after living nearly half a century as a Christian man, I'm still very aware of how much more there is to learn. In fact, as I face new challenges, sometimes I feel I'm still in "boot camp."

This principle also applies to appointing others to leadership positions. As I look back, some of the greatest mistakes I've made were to appoint men to leadership positions who were not adequately prepared. In some instances, the results were disastrous in the way the experience impacted their own lives, their marriages and their families—and the body of Christ. Hopefully, I've learned to be far more discerning and "patient" in fulfilling my own leadership responsibilities.

Joshua's example has helped me greatly—and I'm confident that a study of his life will help you too—no matter what your leadership position as a Christian. It'll help you be a better husband, a better father, a better businessman operating in the secular world, or a better minister as you function in either a lay position or in a staff position.

Joshua's basic training took many years. This was "par for the course" among biblical leaders. God was never in a hurry to give them positions of heavy responsibility. He was concerned that they be adequately prepared. This often required years.

What is unique about Joshua in his early years is his open heart, his willingness to be taught and his spirit of humility. Consequently, he learned his lessons well.

Joshua's Great, Great, Great . . . Grandfather

To understand and appreciate Joshua's place in biblical history, we need to understand his heritage. In fact, what happened in Joshua's adult life relates to a specific promise God made to Abraham centuries before when He called him out of Ur of the Chaldeans.

Abraham's Encounter with God

Though significant events are recorded in the first eleven chapters of the Bible, the unfolding story of redemption actually begins in Genesis 12 with the Abrahamic covenant or contract. At that moment in history, God looked down on sinful and lost humanity. Out of a pagan culture and world that had turned away from Him as the one true God, He chose Abraham, a man who lived in Ur of the Chaldeans.

A Land, a Seed, a Blessing

God made three basic promises to Abraham (originally called Abram). He was going to bless him with a *land*—a permanent home. God also promised Abraham a *seed*—a heritage, a great nation of people. Most importantly, God promised that through Abraham, the whole world would be *blessed* (Gen. 12:1–3). God was referring to a future "son of Abraham," God's eternal Son, Jesus Christ, who would be born in due time and become the Savior for all mankind (Gal. 3:6–9).

History Compressed

Abraham responded to God's call and command. By faith, he entered the land of Canaan (see the map below), and a series of events followed. Looking at biblical history compressed, Abraham eventually had two sons, Ishmael and Isaac (Gen. 16:15;

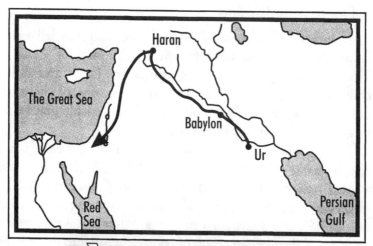

Abraham's Journey

21:2). According to God's plan, Isaac was the chosen heir, and through him, God's promises continued to unfold. Isaac had two sons, Esau and Jacob (25:24–26), and according to God's divine decree, Jacob became the channel God used to continue to carry out His specific promises to Abraham. Jacob eventually had twelve sons, later called the sons of Israel.

The Plot Thickens

At this point in Old Testament history, the plot thickens. Jacob's older sons hated their younger brother, Joseph, because their father favored him. Inventing an evil scheme, they sold him as a slave to a band of Midianites. These slave traders carried Joseph to Egypt where he was sold to Potiphar, the captain of the bodyguard for the king of Egypt (37:28, 36).

This was not the end for Joseph—rather, the beginning. Though he faced some incredible difficulties, he soon became a very successful man and eventually rose to a position of great prominence in Egypt. At age thirty, he was actually the executive leader of the country, reporting directly to the Pharaoh.

A Devastating Famine

Eventually—and ironically—God used Joseph to deliver his family from a devastating famine in the land of Canaan. Through God's providential care, his father, Jacob, and all his children and grandchildren came to live in one of the most productive areas in Egypt. At that time, Joseph graciously forgave his brothers for their sin against him.

For approximately four hundred years, the children of Israel (Jacob's name was changed to Israel—32:28; 35:10) grew into a great nation, just as God had promised Abraham (12:2). However, the kings of Egypt who knew Joseph eventually died (Exod. 1:8), and a Pharaoh came to power who was threatened by this rapidly growing group of people. In order to discourage and demoralize them, he placed burdens on them they could hardly bear.

Deliverance from Egypt

God did not forget his promises to Abraham. In His divine timing, He raised up a great leader named Moses who eventually led the children of Israel out of Egypt. Now a great multitude, they miraculously crossed the Red Sea on dry ground. Though they wandered in the wilderness for forty years because of their sins, God eventually brought them to the edge of the land He had promised Abraham and his descendants so many years before (see the map below).

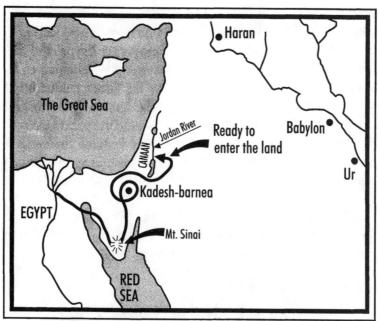

Journey Out of Egypt

The Largest Sandals a Man Has Ever Seen

At this point, Joshua—the man we are about to meet—walked on to God's divine and providential stage as successor to Moses. Because Moses failed to obey on one very important occasion,

God did not allow him to enter the Promised Land. He could see it but he could not cross over the Jordan River. God Himself buried Moses and recorded the following epitaph on his "tombstone": "No prophet has risen in Israel like Moses, whom the LORD knew face to face" (Deut. 34:10, NIV).

Joshua was destined to step into the largest sandals he'd ever had on his feet.

Boot Camp

Joshua was born in Egypt. His father and mother were slaves along with all the children of Israel who had become victims of the Pharaoh—the "new king" who "arose over Egypt" and "did not know Joseph" (Exod. 1:8). As a young lad clinging to his mother's toga, Joshua no doubt saw his father trudge home many nights from the fields, weary and exhausted from working from sunup to sundown under the merciless taskmasters of Egypt. Joshua was born many years after Pharaoh first became threatened by Israel's growth rate, but the inhuman persecution never abated until the day Moses led them out of Egypt.

Obviously, Joshua's early memories were anything but pleasant. When he grew older, he too became a "working" slave. Like any young Hebrew man, there were times when he could have been killed. But in God's providence, he survived.

One Awesome Night

There was one terrible but blessed night Joshua would never forget. It happened when Moses was preparing to lead all Israel out of Egypt. God had already sent a series of nine devastating plagues upon Pharaoh's people. But the tenth plague was the *most devastating.* The Lord was going to take the life of every firstborn in Egypt—including the animals. However, the Lord provided a very unusual but prophetic way for Israelite parents to save the lives of their eldest children. They were to kill a lamb and sprinkle its blood on the doorposts of their homes. "'When

I see the blood,'" the Lord said, "'I will pass over you, and no plague will befall you to destroy you when I strike the land of Egypt'" (12:13).

Joshua evidently was the firstborn as well as the eldest son in his family (1 Chron. 7:27). Neither he, nor any firstborn Israelite, could ever forget that horrific night—or the morning that followed. The mournful wailing and shrieks from Egyptian parents pierced the night air when they discovered that every eldest child had been slain. How thankful Joshua must have been to be among the living and among those who marched triumphantly out of Egypt, following their great leader, Moses.

A Great Mentor

Moses must have already become an ideal role model in Joshua's heart and mind. He knew of Moses' great faith blended with courage as Moses confronted Pharaoh and pronounced judgment on Egypt. Joshua saw the results of that faith and courage as plague after plague came to pass—first, the waters of the Nile changed to blood, followed by the plagues of frogs, gnats, insects, pestilence, boils, hail, locusts, great darkness and, finally, the death of every firstborn. There was, of course, more to come—the greatest miracle yet! Joshua must have stood speechless and breathless when he saw Moses stretch his rod over the Red Sea. The waters parted, allowing Israel to march across on dry ground. And then he saw Moses extend his rod once again over the waters, causing the sea to return to its place, destroying all the Egyptian warriors who followed the Israelites into the midst of the sea.

By this time in his life, Joshua had settled a very important issue—he *knew* and *believed* that the Lord God of Israel was indeed the one true God. And he also knew that Moses was God's appointed leader of Israel.

Joshua soon became Moses' right-hand man. In fact, this special relationship had begun even before they marched out of

Egypt, for we read that Joshua, the son of Nun, was an "attendant of Moses from his youth" (Num. 11:28).

Wilderness Experiences

Moses developed unusual confidence in his young lieutenant. This is demonstrated in several significant events during the wilderness journey from Egypt to Canaan.

Joshua's First Military Assignment

On the way to the Promised Land, the children of Israel faced enemies who resented the intrusion into their territory. At Rephidim (Exod. 17:8–16)—the place where Moses struck the rock and brought forth water—Amalek's army attacked the Israelites. As Moses' military assistant, Joshua led a counterattack and, with God's supernatural assistance, he led his fledgling army of men to their first military victory.

This experience certainly helped prepare Joshua for the challenges he would face in the land of Canaan. His most important lesson was that God was on their side. If they would simply obey Him, they would be victorious over their enemies. Joshua never forgot that experience at Rephidim.

Joshua's Mountaintop Experience

When Israel arrived in the wilderness of Sinai and camped in front of that great mountain, all the people could hear God's voice reverberating from that sacred place. Later, God wrote His laws on tablets of stone and commanded Moses to climb the mountain, enter His presence and receive the Ten Commandments. Responding to God's order, he also took Joshua with him (24:12–13)—not allowing the other leaders in Israel to join them. "'Wait here for us,'" said Moses to the elders, "'until we [Moses and Joshua] return to you'" (v. 14).

The exact details in this story are not clear. It's doubtful that Joshua experienced God's glory to the same degree as Moses, but he did enjoy greater access to the Lord's presence than the other leaders. He alone was allowed to continue up the mountain with Moses. When he was instructed to remain behind, we're not told. But we do know that his exposure to God's presence was second only to Moses'. Joshua was so overwhelmed with Moses' personal relationship with the Lord that at times he would not leave Moses' side: "Thus the LORD used to speak to Moses face to face, just as a man speaks to his friend. When Moses returned to the camp, his servant Joshua, the son of Nun, a young man, would not depart from the tent" (33:11).

What happened in Sinai demonstrates dramatically the unique position Joshua already held as Moses' right-hand man. It also reveals the unique relationship he had with God. All of these experiences were divinely designed by the Lord to prepare Joshua for his future leadership role with Israel. If Joshua had known at the time what God had in store for him, he would have lost perspective. Just knowing he was going to eventually replace Moses would have been far more than he could have handled psychologically. And, if Moses had known before the fact that he was not going to be allowed to lead Israel into the Promised Land, he would have been so disheartened, discouraged, and depressed he could not have gone on.

There is an important lesson here. Only God knows our future, and in His providential timing, He unveils His sovereign plan, which in some incomprehensible way is interrelated and interwoven with our freedom to make choices. Moses' sin and failure was not predetermined by God, but Joshua's unique preparation was! Only an omniscient and sovereign God can design a plan like that!

Joshua's Surveillance Mission

Joshua's opportunity to demonstrate his commitment to his commander-in-chief came when Moses appointed him, along with eleven other men, to enter Canaan to spy out the land (Num. 13:1–14:10). When they returned from their mission, only Joshua and Caleb were positive about entering Canaan. The others were frightened by what they had seen—fortified cities and giant warriors. They instilled this same fear in all Israel, and the whole nation rose up in rebellion against Moses and his brother, Aaron.

At this point, Joshua demonstrated incredible maturity. He, along with Caleb, dared to confront the congregation of the sons of Israel, saying:

> "The land which we passed through to spy out is an exceedingly good land. If the LORD is pleased with us, then He will bring us into this land, and give it to us—a land which flows with milk and honey. Only do not rebel against the LORD; and do not fear the people of the land, for they shall be our prey. Their protection has been removed from them, and the LORD is with us; do not fear them." (Num. 14:7–9)

Sadly, the children of Israel didn't listen. They rose up against Joshua and Caleb and tried to stone them. But, at that moment, God intervened and pronounced judgment on His people. Because of their rebellion, they were destined to wander in the wilderness for forty years until all of that adult generation died. None of them could enter Canaan—except Joshua and Caleb—and Joshua, as Moses' successor, would lead the new generation across Jordan.

Joshua's experience as a spy taught him more important lessons as a military leader. This was just another course in the "wilderness school" that God had designed to prepare him for his future responsibilities. Joshua had passed every test, and in another forty years he would be ready to lead Israel into Canaan.

A Unique "Medal of Honor"

At some point in time—perhaps after the twelve tribes returned from their mission in Canaan—Joshua received a "medal of honor" bestowed on very few people in God's great army.

Originally, his name was Hoshea (or Oshea, Num. 13:8), but Moses changed his name to Joshua (Num. 13:16). Like Barnabas in the New Testament, the reason for this name change is explained in the names themselves. The apostles changed Joseph's name to "Barnabas," which means "Son of Encouragement," simply because he was such an unselfish, caring leader during the early days of the church.

Moses' reasons were similar to the apostles. Hoshea means "salvation." From a human point of view, "Hoshea" would be Israel's savior. But Joshua means "the Lord is salvation." From a divine point of view, *God* would lead Israel into Canaan. Though the Lord would definately use what this young man had learned at Moses' side—in Egypt, in the war against Amalek, on Mount Sinai, his experience as a spy and his subsequent and frightening encounter with Israel when they tried to kill him—yet it was God who would indeed lead Israel into Canaan. It was He who would roll back the waters of Jordan, who would cause the walls of Jericho to fall down, and enable Israel to defeat the people of Ai. It was God who would fell the giants in Canaan. Consequently, Moses changed Hoshea's name to Joshua to emphasize and illustrate that God alone was Israel's salvation.

Joshua learned this lesson well! In God's time, he became ready to allow the Lord to use his abilities and skills and all that he had learned during his years of preparation.

Becoming God's Man Today

Principles to Live By

There are several important lessons we can all learn from this introductory look at Joshua's preparation for leadership in Israel.

Principle 1. It takes time to become prepared to be a faithful leader of others.

Joshua's prominence in Israel came only after many years of faithfulness, both to the Lord and His commandments, as well as to Moses, God's appointed leader. Joshua proved himself worthy of trust.

Many men today want to bypass the process of demonstrating faithfulness over a period of time. In this sense, we're a product of our culture. Our tendency is to desire instant recognition, instant prominence, instant responsibility in fulfilling important leadership roles in God's great army—the Body of Christ. Furthermore, many of us who are already in leadership positions are too quick to appoint people to positions of important spiritual responsibility.

What God Is Looking For

Paul instructed Timothy to avoid appointing spiritual leaders in the church too quickly (1 Tim. 5:22). Earlier in this letter, Paul had charged Timothy to make sure that those desiring spiritual leadership in the church

➤ had a good reputation

➤ were morally pure

➤ demonstrated a well-ordered philosophy of life

➤ were self-disciplined

➤ had respect and credibility among others

➤ were unselfish in the use of their material possessions

➤ were not in bondage to fleshly appetites

➤ were sensitive

➤ were nondefensive

➤ were kind and gentle

➤ were proper leaders of their own families.

Finally, Paul stated that a Christian who is given a high level of spiritual leadership responsibility must not be a new Christian because of the temptation toward pride (1 Tim. 3:1–7).[1]

Some Personal Reflections

As I look over my years in the ministry, particularly as a pastor, I now see that one of the mistakes I made in my initial years of experience was to appoint men to leadership positions in the church who were not ready.

Some of these men didn't have enough experience to handle their assigned responsibilities. The reason is pure and simple. They were too young. Where they were in their chronological development didn't match the demands of their leadership roles.

Some other men were not qualified—not because of age, but because they lacked experience. They had not proven themselves in the difficult seasons of life. In some instances, I saw their marriages collapse because of the added pressures.

I remember well Jim and Mary (not their real names). Before Jim's appointment to a lay pastoral role in the church, several people had indicated they had heard reports that this couple had experienced marital problems in the past. In fact, my wife told me she had some concerns based on what she had observed.

One lesson I've learned over the years is to listen more carefully to my wife, who has proved to be a very godly and perceptive person when it comes to evaluating character. Unfortunately, I did not investigate Jim's marital situation as thoroughly as I should have. Sadly, this marriage ended in divorce. Though this might have happened anyway, I'm confident the pressures of spiritual leadership added to the circumstances that eventually ruptured this marriage permanently.

Learning to Ask the Tough Questions

One of the things I've learned about myself is that I find it difficult to ask people the really difficult questions. One reason for this tendency is that I don't want to offend people. Furthermore, I find it difficult to risk personal rejection.

Another reason is that I find it easy to believe in others. In fact, one of my close associates once remarked—"Gene, your greatest strength is to *trust people.* However, your greatest weakness is to *trust people you shouldn't trust.*"

Over the years, this statement has proved to be true. However, I've also learned through experience to be more cautious, guarded, and discriminating in the selection and appointment of leaders. I still find it very easy to trust people, but I've also learned to ask more penetrating questions. I've also learned to take other people's evaluations more seriously.

Principle 2. As Christian men, we must realize there is a unique balance between dependence on God and confidence in ourselves.

Without question, God used Joshua—*the man*—as a means to achieve His goals. But Joshua knew it was God Himself who would guide and direct Israel. It was His power that rolled back the waters of Jordan, His strength that caused the walls of Jericho to collapse, His wisdom that enabled Joshua to strategize against the enemies of Israel.

This is a divine mystery. God *does* use us—our faithfulness, our commitment, our human capacities and capabilities. But in reality, without Him we'll accomplish little—and what we do accomplish may turn out to be "wood, hay, straw" (1 Cor. 3:12).

Paul issued a solemn warning to the Corinthian churches regarding this possibility. We must:

Build Carefully!

According to the grace of God which was given to me, as a wise master builder I have laid the foundation, and another builds on it. But let each one take heed how he builds on it. For no other foundation can anyone lay than that which is laid, which is Jesus Christ. Now if anyone builds on this foundation with gold, silver, precious stones, *wood, hay, straw,* each one's work will become manifest; for the Day will declare it, because it will be revealed by fire; and the fire will test each one's work, of what sort it is. If anyone's work which he has built on it endures, he will receive a reward. If anyone's work is burned, he will suffer loss; but he himself will be saved, yet so as through fire. (1 Cor. 3:10–15, NKJV)

To build carefully is a very straightforward exhortation to all of us as Christian men—not only regarding our ministry in the church, but in our marriages and families. We can't face life's challenges in our own strength and be ultimately successful. On the one hand, God wants to use all of our human resources. Yet, He is the One who enables us to succeed. Thus, Paul penned the following additional exhortations:

It's Christ in Me

I have been crucified with Christ; and it is no longer I who live, but Christ lives in me; and the life which I now live in the flesh I live by faith in the Son of God, who loved me, and delivered Himself up for me. (Gal. 2:20)

Strengthened with His Power

For this reason, I bow my knees before the Father, from whom every family in heaven and on earth derives its name, that He would grant you, according to the riches of His glory, to be strengthened with power through His Spirit in the inner man. (Eph. 3:14–16)

The Armor of God

Finally, be strong in the Lord, and in the strength of His might . . . Therefore, take up the full armor of God, that you may be able to resist in the evil day, and having done everything, to stand firm. (Eph. 6:10, 13)

Principle 3. We must begin to serve God now in order to be prepared for future responsibility.

It *does* take time to become prepared to handle important spiritual responsibilities. However, that time should be spent faithfully serving God in less demanding roles and learning from more mature and experienced men. In this sense, we all need mentors. This was Joshua's strength. Moses was his example, his role model, and his spiritual shepherd.

Note also that Joshua served faithfully without even knowing that someday he would take over Moses' leadership role. This implies another reason why God chose him—and used him! Not only did he learn his lessons well but his motives were pure.

Points of Action

This life response and the ones to follow are designed to help you personalize the lessons we will be learning from Joshua's life and experiences. Think carefully and seriously at this point. Unless you take this final step you'll miss what God intended when He recorded the life experiences of men like Joshua.

What about your life? Where are you in the process of demonstrating your commitment both to God and to other members of Christ's Body? Have you been faithful in the "little things"—and in the long haul?

Length of Time Is Not the Most Important Point

The amount of time involved in Joshua's preparation is not the crucial issue in this story. In fact, there's no way to set absolutely the amount of time that may be involved in a person's preparation to serve. Sometimes God shortcuts this process considerably.

As I think back, I now know that God did this in my own life. I was only twenty years old when I walked through a very difficult wilderness experience. I focused on men rather than Christ. In the process, I became horribly disillusioned. My heart was filled with doubts about who I really was, what I really believed, and what life was all about! It was a very difficult time.

I now know that God used this period in my life to prepare me for my future role—one that I could not have ever anticipated. Little did I realize that I would be the youngest man to ever join the faculty at Moody Bible Institute in Chicago. In a very short time, God dealt with some areas in my life I didn't know were problems—spiritual pride, religious prejudice, theological confusion! God definitely shortcut the process of growth in my life. Painful? Very! But necessary if I was to succeed in a very important leadership role.

A Lifetime Experience

It does take time to grow and mature—since it's a lifetime adventure. It also means faithfully fulfilling the tasks God gives us along the way. Success at one level prepares us for success at another level. It is only as we pass these tests that God entrusts us with more responsibility.

Although men can build great kingdoms, achieve great goals, and even change the direction of history—seemingly without acknowledging God at all—it is only those who rely on God who achieve goals that really make a difference in the light of eternity.

What about you? Are you primarily concerned about the here and now—your immediate success, your reputation, your material accomplishments? If you are, you'll probably be successful by the world's standards. But in God's eyes you may be achieving very little. Remember the words of Jesus: "'But seek first His kingdom, and His righteousness; and all these things shall be added to you'" (Matt. 6:33).

This was Joshua's experience. And at the end of his life God surely said, "Well done, good and faithful slave" (Matt. 25:21). Consider this great tribute recorded at the time of his death: "And Israel served the LORD all the days of Joshua and all the days of the elders who survived Joshua, and had known all the deeds of the LORD which He had done for Israel" (Josh. 24:31).

A Man's Man Is a Godly Man

As you evaluate the following principles, pray and ask the Holy Spirit to impress on your heart one lesson you need to apply more effectively in your life. Then write out a specific goal. For example, you may recognize that you are impatient. You want a significant leadership position *now*. You're not willing to wait for God's timing or to develop certain character qualities that will make you ready for a particular responsibility.

> It takes time to become prepared to be a faithful leader.

> As Christian men, we must realize there is a unique balance between dependence on God and confidence in ourselves.

> We must begin to serve God now in order to be prepared for future responsibility.

Set a Goal

With God's help, I will begin immediately to carry out the following goal in my life:

_____

_____

_____

_____

Memorize the Following Scripture

Not that I have already obtained it, or have already become perfect, but I press on in order that I may lay hold of that for which also I was laid hold of by Christ Jesus. Brethren, I do not regard myself as having laid hold of it yet; but one thing I do: forgetting what lies behind and reaching forward to what lies ahead, I press on toward the goal for the prize of the upward call of God in Christ Jesus.

PHILIPPIANS 3:12–14

Chapter 2

A Call to Courage

Read Joshua 1:1–18

Suppose the board of directors of a large corporation selected you to be the next president. But even as they were appointing you to this leadership role, they made the statement—in your presence—that the previous president was irreplaceable. Furthermore, you knew from your own experience that what they were saying was absolutely true. You had worked side by side, day after day, with the previous president. You witnessed his leadership ability. You saw his wisdom and his courage. More importantly, you observed firsthand his faith in God. There was no way to feel that you could ever measure up to that man in any respect!

How would you feel? No matter how much the board of directors tried to reassure you of their confidence in you and that you could do the job, the awesome reality of the previous man's track record would haunt you. And the fact that you could never quite measure up would probably threaten you every morning as you left for the office.

Some Vivid Memories

In many respects, this might describe Joshua's feelings. But his predicament was intensified many times over.

Moses' Great Accomplishments

Moses had marched into Pharaoh's court and pronounced judgment on the Egyptians. Joshua was with him as this great man of God boldly led the children of Israel toward the Red Sea. He watched in amazement as Moses held out his rod and parted that sea.

Joshua also accompanied Moses up the mountain that was aglow with fire and resonant with thunder. He knew Moses had communicated with God "face to face" (Exod. 33:11). He had seen this great leader of Israel come down from the mountain with his face reflecting the glory of God.

Throughout the wilderness wanderings, Joshua had looked on in astonishment as God used Moses as a human instrument to bring water out of the rock to quench Israel's thirst. He had seen Moses sweeten the waters of Marah and feed the children of Israel with quail and manna from heaven.

Joshua knew all these things about his predecessor. To try to assume Moses' role as the leader of the children of Israel would have been a threatening experience for any human being.

Facing Incredible Rejection

Probably even more frightening to Joshua than living in the shadow of Moses' great achievements would be his awareness of the number of times that the fickle children of Israel rejected their leader.

How could he help but have vivid memories of the times the children of Israel rose up against Moses, even to the point of threatening to kill him when he would not allow them to return to Egypt? And how could he forget that fearful moment when he and Caleb returned from spying out the land of Canaan and dared to confront those who defied God and refused to go in and take the land immediately? Joshua would never forget the numerous occasions when the unbelief of Israel was beyond belief itself.

And now Moses was gone! Joshua stood alone with the tremendous responsibility of taking over the leadership of this great multitude of unpredictable and often fickle people.

"Be Strong and Courageous"

There's no doubt about it! Joshua faced one of the greatest challenges of his life. Though the role he found himself in as leader of Israel was no surprise, the reality of it all suddenly crushed in on him. Questions flooded his mind. How could he handle this great a responsibility? What if the children of Israel did not accept him as Moses' successor? What if he failed? What if the children of Israel rebelled?

The Reality Was Awesome

God understood Joshua's dilemma. The Lord never gives us a task without providing the resources and help to carry out the responsibility—which is dramatically illustrated in God's words to Joshua in the introductory verses of the first chapter of the book that bears his name. Previously, the Lord had spoken *directly* to Moses. Now He spoke *directly* and reassuringly to Joshua. "'Just as I *spoke to Moses*,'" the Lord said, and "'Just as I *have been with Moses*, I will be with you'" (Josh. 1:3, 5).*

Isn't it encouraging that God understood Joshua's human weaknesses? This new leader in Israel was almost overwhelmed by the tremendous responsibility that had fallen on his shoulders. Even though God had prepared him ahead of time, the reality of what lay before him was awesome. Consequently, God charged Joshua to "be strong and courageous"—a phrase that appears four times in this opening chapter (vv. 6–7, 9, 18).

His Fears Were Understandable

Joshua's fears are indeed comprehensible. After all, he had been chosen to follow in the footsteps of one of God's most powerful and distinguished leaders of all time (Deut. 34:9–12).

---

*Hereafter, the author has italicized words and phrases in Scripture passages for emphasis.

And even though Joshua had proven himself again and again and had been informed on several occasions that he was going to take over Moses' responsibilities, when the moment finally arrived, it was an intimidating challenge.

Again, these responses are predictable, particularly for a man who really understood what lay ahead of him. Calvin once noted: "Even some of the bravest men, although fully prepared beforehand, either stand still or hesitate when the thing needs to be done."

Joshua Was a Brave Man

Had he not served as a successful military leader during the wilderness journey? Wasn't he one of the two spies (out of the twelve) who eagerly wanted to enter and conquer the land forty years earlier, even though from a human point of view it looked impossible?

Joshua also had been well prepared for this moment. His "boot camp" and "field experience" were unmatched among Israel's top men. Earlier Moses had proclaimed in the presence of all Israel, affirming his confidence and faith in Joshua:

"*Be strong and courageous*, for you shall go with this people into the land . . . And the LORD is the one who goes ahead of you; He will be with you. He will not fail you or forsake you. Do not fear, or be dismayed." (Deut. 31:7–8)

But . . . When the Moment Finally Arrived

Just before his death, Moses "laid his hands" on Joshua and commissioned him for this new task—again in the presence of all the sons of Israel (34:9). But even in view of his obvious bravery, the preparation he had for the task, and Moses' confidence in him, when the time finally arrived to take over the responsibility, Joshua was suddenly overtaken with fear. He understood only too well the awesomeness of God's charge and what lay ahead of him.

Ignorance Is Bliss

A group of university students from Toronto had gone up to Georgian Bay for a fishing trip. They hired a boat and a captain to take them out into the bay. That morning, a storm broke. The captain, an old tar, sat at the helm with a worried look on his face. The students laughed at his fear and through their laughter declared, "We are not afraid!" The old sea dog looked at them and said, "Yes, you are too ignorant to be afraid."

Joshua was not ignorant of what lay ahead. Anyone who understands the threatening dynamics involved at this moment in Joshua's life should be able to understand—at least somewhat—his predicament. How would you or I feel about replacing a leader whom God had publicly declared could not be replaced? In position, yes! But qualitatively, no! The Scriptures declare: "Since then no prophet has risen in Israel like Moses, whom the LORD knew face to face" (34:10). Though written from the perspective of history, Joshua obviously knew in his heart that there would never be another man like Moses.

Conditions for Success

The Lord did more than reassure Joshua of His presence and power (Josh. 1:7–9). He also spelled out very specifically and clearly the conditions for successfully taking the land. God left no "ands," "ifs," and "buts" undefined.

Obedience to God's Word

The Lord gave Joshua five direct commands, all related to His laws. Though similar, they clearly outline God's conditions for successfully taking the land of Canaan:

➤ "Be careful to do according to all the law [and]"

➤ "Do not turn from it to the right or to the left" (v. 7);

➤ "This book of the law shall not depart from your mouth, but
  . . ."

➤ "You shall meditate on it day and night [and]"

➤ "Be careful to do according to all that is written in it" (v. 8).

Comprehend, Practice and Communicate

God made it clear to Joshua that if he consistently obeyed these commands, he would be successful and prosperous (vv. 7–8). These interrelated commands can be summarized as follows:

First, Joshua had to make sure that he knew and *understood* the law that God had already given to Moses. To achieve this goal, he must review it regularly and consistently—meditating "on it day and night."

Second, Joshua had to *practice* the law of God in his own personal and public life—not turning "from it to the right or to the left." He could not lead Israel to obey God without exemplifying obedience in his own life.

Third, and perhaps most important, Joshua had to boldly and confidently *communicate* God's Word to the children of Israel. The law of God must never depart from his mouth.

Overcoming Fear

As God gave these commands, He encouraged Joshua to be "strong and courageous" (vv. 6–7, 9). Becoming even more specific, the Lord said: "Do not *tremble* or be *dismayed*" (v. 9b). Joshua was never to shy away from his responsibility. He shouldn't fear the children of Israel and allow himself to become intimidated. He was to be bold and strong like Moses and to speak with the very authority of the Lord God of Israel.

Conditional vs. Unconditional Promises

Israel's success in taking the land was clearly conditioned on their obedience to the Word of God. But this raises a very important question. Wasn't the land promised to Israel unconditionally?

What about God's land promise to Abraham (Gen. 12:1–3; 13:15, 17; 15:18–19; 17:8; 28:13; 35:12)? How can you have conditions attached to an unconditional promise?

The Scriptures may sound contradictory regarding the "land promise," but they are not when we understand God's complete plan for Israel. First, we must realize that God's land promise to Israel *is* unconditional. However, not only is it unconditional, it is also *literal*.

Literal Soil, Literal Distance, Literal Promises

Some Christians try to spiritualize this truth. Frankly, I have difficulty understanding God's reference to "dirt" and "distance" if it is not a literal promise. Abraham was to walk up and down the land. This was *literal soil* (13:17). God told Abraham to look north and south and east and west, and then said, "For all the land that you see, I will give it to you and to your descendants forever" (vv. 14–15). This is *literal distance*. Consequently, these were literal promises to Abraham and his children.

Occupation vs. Ownership

As we read about Israel in the Scriptures, we must not miss a very important principle: Ownership of the land of Israel is unconditional. It belongs to the children of Israel and eventually God will give them all of it! However, they will not possess or occupy it totally and enjoy it until they are perfectly obedient to all of the Lord's commands.

"Lock, Stock, and Barrel"

This unconditional promise to Israel, then, still stands. Furthermore, the conditions are also a reality. But one of these days, perhaps soon, they'll have it all—lock, stock, and barrel. It will happen as God said it would because God will do it! He will gather the people of Israel from all nations and bring them back into their own land. He will "sprinkle clean water" on them. He will give them "a new heart and put a new spirit within" them. This is what God meant when He revealed His will to Israel through Ezekiel the prophet:

> "I will put My Spirit within you and cause you to walk in My statutes, and you will be careful to observe My ordinances. And you will live in the land that I gave to your forefathers; so you will be My people, and I will be your God." (Ezek. 36:27–28)

Meanwhile, Back in Joshua's Day . . .

In this study, we'll see that Joshua cannot be faulted for his role in Israel's history. Under his leadership they had victory after victory and eventually experienced rest in the land. God was true to His promise of success, and Joshua 1:7–9 records that promise: As long as Israel met His conditions and obeyed His Word, they had success and were victorious wherever they went.

Then we read in the last chapter of the Book of Joshua: "And Israel served the LORD *all the days of Joshua* and all the days of the elders who survived Joshua, and had known all the deeds of the LORD which He had done for Israel" (24:31).

Trust and Obey, There's No Other Way

Joshua was very encouraged and strengthened because of God's direct communication. He wasted no time responding to God's charge. In Joshua 1:10–18, we are able to read how he first assumed the leadership role by calling together the officers and leaders of the people. He then issued a command which can be divided into two sections:

> ➤ First, he directed his words to all of the children of Israel (vv. 10–11). They were to get ready to cross over Jordan to take possession of the land of Canaan.

> ➤ Second, he spoke specifically to the Reubenites, the Gadites and the half-tribe of Manasseh. He reviewed for them what had happened under Moses' leadership. Israel had captured

a parcel of land on the side of Jordan opposite Canaan which Moses had promised them. But there was one important condition. The Reubenite, Gadite and Manasseh warriors were to act as "shock troops" and pass over Jordan ahead of the rest of Israel (v. 14). When the task was finished and they had helped take possession of the land, they could return to the other side of Jordan and settle permanently into the land Moses had promised them (Deut. 3:8–19).

Self-confidence and God-confidence

After Joshua had reviewed Moses' conditions, everyone agreed (Josh. 1:16–18). They responded willingly and with eagerness and said, "'Just as we obeyed Moses in all things, so we will obey you'" (v. 17). They then reassured Joshua that anyone who rebelled and did not follow Joshua's command would "be put to death." They then showed their full support when they said, "Only be strong and courageous" (v. 18).

This positive response was the reassurance Joshua needed. From this point on, he "felt" like their leader. There seemed to be no questions, doubts, or hesitancy. His fear and trembling turned into boldness, a steady hand, and a quick stride that demonstrated an attitude of self-confidence blended with a strong faith in God.

Becoming God's Man Today

Principles to Live By

Principle 1. We too can, and must, "be strong and courageous"— whatever our responsibilities or our position in life.

As businessmen, as husbands, as fathers, as church leaders, and as active members of Christ's body, we *can* face our responsibilities with confidence and assurance. Most importantly, the basis of that security lies not in ourselves, but in the fact that the same help that was available to Joshua is available to each one of us.

God Understands!

Like Joshua, we all have human weaknesses—fears, anxieties, and feelings of inadequacy. But, God understood all of these problems in Joshua's life and reassured him and helped him rise above his frustrating circumstances.

God also understands our humanness. He made us. He knows us. He sympathizes with us. There is no struggle with which He does not identify. He does not stand over us ready to condemn us in moments of weakness. Rather, He is reaching out to help us, to reassure us—just as He did for Joshua!

A Wonderful Reality

God's great act of love in reaching out to us in sending Jesus Christ makes this truth possible on an ongoing basis. Consider the wonderful reality described in the Hebrews' letter:

> Since then we have a great high priest who has passed through the heavens, Jesus the Son of God, let us hold fast our confession. For we do not have a high priest who cannot sympathize with our weaknesses, but one who has been tempted in all things as we are, yet without sin. Let us therefore draw near with confidence to the throne of grace, that we may receive mercy and may find grace to help in time of need. (Heb. 4:14–16)

God's Revealed Truth

Our authority—like Joshua's—is based on the Word of God. The Lord dealt with Joshua's fear by reviewing for him His previous promises to Israel regarding the land of Canaan. Furthermore, He charged Joshua to become thoroughly familiar with His law, to apply it to his own life and then to clearly and consistently communicate it to all the children of Israel.

All Men Have Fears—Including Pastors

Paul repeated the same basic instructions to Timothy, a young spiritual leader who oftentimes experienced fear in carrying out his responsibilities. Very early in Paul's second letter to Timothy, he stated: "For God has not given us a spirit of timidity, but of power and love and discipline" (2 Tim. 1:7). Later in the same letter he wrote: "Be strong in the grace that is in Christ Jesus. . . . Be diligent to present yourself approved to God as a workman who does not need to be ashamed, handling accurately the word of truth" (2:1, 15). And still later, Paul wrote: "I solemnly charge . . . : preach the word; be ready in season and out of season; reprove, rebuke, exhort, with great patience and instruction" (4:1–2).

After serving as a professor for nearly twenty years (thirteen years at Moody Bible Institute and seven years at Dallas Theological Seminary), I faced a wonderful but challenging opportunity to lead out in launching a new church. What made this opportunity somewhat threatening was that the families who asked me to serve as their founding pastor had in mind a certain kind of church. They wanted to launch this new ministry with a commitment to supracultural biblical functions and principles—not to particular cultural forms and patterns. In other words, they wanted to go back to the basics of New Testament Christianity and then develop structures relevant to our culture without compromising the absolutes of the Bible. In this sense, they wanted to follow the apostle Paul's example—to "become all things to all men" so that "by all means" we might "save some" (1 Cor. 9:22).

What made this challenge threatening is that I had never gone through this process before. I had lots of experience functioning and leading in a traditional church setting. And I felt very confident as a professor—but, would I be successful as a church planting pastor who was leading a group of people to do something none of us had ever done before?

To be perfectly honest, I experienced a great deal of anxiety. What if this experiment failed? What would people's reaction be? What about those who would criticize me because they didn't understand?

I believe I felt a little of what Joshua felt when God appointed him leader of Israel. True, his leadership role was many times more threatening and demanding than mine. However, even though our degree of responsibility may vary greatly, our emotional responses are often very similar. But God understands! He met Joshua's need—and He met my need in the same way. Today that initial church which we call Fellowship Bible Church has multiplied many times. God was faithful! When He calls us to do a job, He'll also give us the courage to respond. That's certainly what happened to Joshua.

Principle 2. Obedience brings blessing.

Martin Luther once said that "he who walks according to God's Word acts wisely and happily, but he who goes according to his own head acts unwisely and to no profit."

This simple but profound statement reflects a major lesson in the first chapter of Joshua. God shared with this new leader of Israel a very important secret to successful spiritual living and leadership—obedience to His Word brings blessing.

Rest assured that this is an ongoing promise throughout Scripture and applicable to all believers. And where it is not stated specifically, it is assumed. God honors obedience to His Word. Thus Paul wrote: "And do not be conformed to this world, but be transformed by the renewing of your mind, that you may prove what the will of God is, that which is good and acceptable and perfect" (Rom. 12:2).

Remember too that blessings from God are not only temporal but eternal. The most important reward for obedience to God's Word will be His "well done, thou good and faithful servant" (Matt. 25:21, KJV).

Principle 3. God will never forsake us.

"'Be strong and courageous! Do not tremble or be dismayed, for *the LORD your God is with you wherever you go*'" (Josh. 1:9). These must have been the most reassuring words that God spoke to Joshua. The Lord Himself promised to be his continual companion and divine resource.

Jesus made a very similar statement when He gave the Great Commission. "'Lo,'" He promised, "'I am with you always, even to the end of the age'" (Matt. 28:20).

Great Is Thy Faithfulness

There is One we can trust. We read in the Hebrews' letter, "He who promised is faithful" (Heb. 10:23). And the Old Testament prophet said beautifully, "The LORD's lovingkindnesses indeed never cease, for His compassions never fail. They are new every morning; great is Thy faithfulness" (Lam. 3:22–23). Christians have sung confidently for years William M. Runyan's great hymn of faith, "Great Is Thy Faithfulness."

Marching Forward

Life is filled with threatening situations. To act responsibly and proactively calls for daily courage—in our marriages, in our families, in our dealings with others, and in our churches.

The business world particularly is highly competitive and filled with all sorts of challenges. One of those challenges is to live ethically and honestly, especially if our competitors march to a different drumbeat—a lifestyle directed by values that run counter to biblical standards. But there are other challenges that call for courage, even if there is no conflict in values—challenges that threaten us because we're not sure we'll be successful. And no one, of course, wants to fail at anything!

One of our greatest temptations as men is to allow our egos to control us to the point that we try to solve problems all by ourselves. After all, this is the "American way!" To admit we need help is to admit weakness. We've come a long way in our spiritual growth when we accept that we *do* need God—and others. The Lord established this principle even before sin entered the world when He announced that "it is not good for the man to be alone; I will make him a helper suitable for him" (Gen. 2:18).

Points of Action

Following are some "Points of Action"—questions that will help all of us isolate areas that intimidate us.

➤ Am I fearful and anxious? Do I feel inadequate? Remember that you're not alone! Many of God's greatest leaders have experienced these feelings. But more important, God wants you to be "strong and courageous." And He has given you resources to achieve this goal.

➤ Do I have a correct view of God's loving concern for me—that He wants to meet my needs if I'll just let Him?

➤ Do I take seriously the Word of God and its promises? Do I realize this is the greatest source of encouragement? Do I consult the Bible regularly? Do I meditate upon it? Do I obey it? Do I draw strength from it to carry out my responsibilities—since my authority is indeed based on God's authority?

➤ Do I truly believe that obedience to God's Word will bring blessing, now and eternally?

➤ Do I really believe that God is with me—that He has not forsaken me and He never will?

A Man's Man Is a Godly Man

Reread the questions under Points of Action. As you do, ask the Holy Spirit to impress on your heart one lesson you need to apply more specifically in your life. Then write out a specific goal. For example, you may feel fearful and anxious. You feel that you are all alone with feelings of inadequacy.

Set a Goal

With God's help, I will begin immediately to carry out the following goal in my life:

_____

_____

_____

Memorize the Following Scripture

"This book of the law shall not depart from your mouth, but you shall meditate on it day and night, so that you may be careful to do according to all that is written in it; for then you will make your way prosperous, and then you will have success."

JOSHUA 1:8

Chapter 3

An Encounter with a Prostitute
Read Joshua 2:1–24

I was reared in a very religious subculture and attended a very "pietistic" church. In reality, my church was legalistic, which is not true biblical piety. But I did not know that then. In fact, I was controlled by spiritual pride at that time and couldn't recognize the difference. Somehow I felt my religious background and heritage gave me a special claim to God's grace and love. In short, I felt I was better than other people who did not attend *my* church.

One day I suddenly awakened to the fact that there were other Christians, outside of my particular circle of friends, who were far more spiritual than I was. Though some of them had not had as much religious training as I, their faith was much stronger and more dynamic. They were more faithful in living up to the light they had.

The Old Testament Hall of Faith

In many respects this is what Joshua and the children of Israel discovered about Rahab the harlot, who lived in Jericho. Though she grew up and lived in a totally pagan and idolatrous culture, she responded in faith when she heard about the God of Israel. In certain respects, she was more responsive spiritually than some of the Israelites. The Lord honored her faith and—what may be a surprise to some—included her in the Old Testament hall of faith in the New Testament.

No woman in all the pages of Scripture stands out as an example of great faith and an object of God's redeeming grace more than Rahab. She's mentioned by the author of Hebrews in the same company of such greats as Noah, Abraham, Isaac, Jacob, Joseph, and Moses—all of whom were commended for their faith. We read: "*By faith Rahab the harlot* did not perish along with those who were disobedient, after she had welcomed the spies in peace" (Heb. 11:31).

How did a prostitute find her way into the Old Testament hall of faith? Read the second chapter of Joshua, and you'll discover the answer.

Rahab lived in Jericho—an idolatrous and immoral Canaanite city. But in the midst of this den of iniquity, she came to know the one true God.

A Secret Mission

There seem to be two basic reasons why Joshua sent spies into the land of Canaan. The first is *military.* Thus Joshua issued the order: "Go, view the land, especially Jericho" (2:1). Israel's new leader wanted to know more about the land, particularly the attitudes of the Canaanites and what they knew about the battle plans of the children of Israel.

Taking No Chances

Interestingly, Joshua sent only two spies into the land of Canaan. Was this a reflection of his own experience years earlier when he was sent as one of twelve? Only he and Caleb had returned with a positive report. The other ten were negative and infected the whole nation of Israel with attitudes of unbelief.

Joshua was taking no chances this time. He was highly selective! Two would do—two men in whom he had confidence to give him an accurate report of the situation, who would not be intimidated by the enemy's military strength and their large fortified cities (Num. 13:28).

God's Love for a Prostitute

The second reason Joshua sent spies into Canaan was *providential*, probably known at this moment only in the mind of God. From a divine perspective, this reason was far more important than Joshua's military interests. A woman and her whole family lived in Jericho who had come to believe in the living and true God, and they needed protection and deliverance. Consequently, most of chapter 2 is given to the story of this woman's faith.

An Incredible Surveillance System

The author of the Book of Joshua wasted no time focusing in on the primary subject of this chapter. Immediately we read: "So they went and came into the house of a harlot whose name was Rahab, and lodged there" (2:1).

Shortly after Joshua's spies entered Rahab's house, men from Jericho also entered. They had been sent by the king and their mission was to capture the two spies from Israel.

How did the king in Jericho know so much?

➤ He was aware that Joshua's men had entered Rahab's house.

➤ He knew they were together and had not split up.

➤ He knew they were "sons of Israel."

➤ He also knew the exact arrival time—that very night.

➤ He knew their purpose—"to search out the land" (vv. 2–3).

Today we use "spy satellites" and video monitors to discover this kind of detailed information. But even the kings of Canaan had set up a tremendous security system. Their own spies were watching every move the children of Israel made. They evidently knew when the spies left the camp on the other side of Jordan.

They must have seen them cross over the river and then followed their every move. Obviously they knew when they entered the city of Jericho and they followed them directly to Rahab's "place of business."

All of this information was conveyed to the king of Jericho at regular intervals. When he learned that the spies had entered Rahab's house, he immediately ordered their capture.

Rahab's Test of Faith

When the king's men arrived at Rahab's house to take the two spies into custody, she had already hidden them on her roof under stalks of flax—as if she already knew that her home would be searched (vv. 1–7). Why this concern? Why this eagerness to protect the sons of Israel? Why the willingness to take a chance on her own life should the spies be discovered? All of these questions point to one basic answer: *Rahab had already changed her allegiance!*

Rahab's "White Lie"

Rahab definitely lied to the men of Jericho—which seems to be one of those situations where telling a falsehood was acceptable to God. This happened before when the Lord honored the Hebrew midwives in Egypt who lied to the Pharaoh. Rather than killing all the boys that were born, as the king had ordered, they let them live. And when the king asked why these boys weren't killed, they reported that the Hebrew mothers gave birth to their babies prematurely, before they could arrive on the scene to help them. The facts were that these women saved these boys because "they feared God." And because of this "godly fear," the Lord "was good to the midwives" (Exod. 1:20).

Just so, God was "good to Rahab!"

We must also remember that Rahab had grown up in a pagan city where the normal lifestyle was lying, cheating, and all forms of immorality. She was a prostitute by profession. She had worshiped the false gods of Canaan. Her knowledge of the one true God only recently had come into focus. In this sense, Rahab was responding to the light she had. And God honored her faith. She passed the test. In lying about the spies, she was literally willing to take a chance on her own life.

Responding to the Light She Had

Rahab was ahead of many of the children of Israel—even though their light was greater. They had seen miracle after miracle, whereas Rahab had only heard about them. The children of Israel had received God's law by His direct revelation to Moses, whereas Rahab only heard indirectly about God's will.

Even with all this light, Israel turned their backs on God again and again, indulging in horrible sins. It appears that God was giving greater attention to Rahab's faith because she was more faithful to the light she had—dim as it was. Compared to Israel, her faith was greater. And she proved it by risking her life for the people of God. In this case, God looked beyond her human weaknesses and saw where she was coming from, and where she was heading.

A Great Measure of Faith

The degree of Rahab's faith is seen by her willingness to hide the spies in her home. She certainly knew about the king's surveillance system. Her risk was great. As we have seen, the king's system was so effective that his men followed the two spies' every move—from the time they left camp until they entered Rahab's home. How easy it would be for the king's men to discover two men on a rooftop! And this would probably mean death for her and perhaps her whole family.

The Miracle of "Mental Blindness"

Why would the king's men suddenly believe that Rahab was telling the truth when she told them the spies had left? Why didn't they search the house before running out into the darkness? On the human side, these men may have simply assumed that *no one* would protect spies from Israel. After all, everyone in Jericho was at risk—including Rahab!

From a divine perspective however, this was a miracle. How else can we explain that the king's tightly controlled and highly effective spy network broke down? God was honoring Rahab's faith. She had passed the test. She dared to believe that this God she had heard about would protect her. And God did not let her down!

Simple Theology: A Strong Faith

Rahab's willingness to risk her life to protect the men of Israel is strong evidence that she had already changed her way of life. But her statement of faith in chapter 2, verses 8 to 11, clearly demonstrates the simple theology that was guiding her behavior.

After the men of Jericho left to pursue Israel's spies, "She came up to them on the roof" (v. 8). Note the certainty with which she spoke to these men—"'I *know*,'" she said, "'that the LORD has given you the land'" (v. 9). Rahab had seen the fear of her own people in Jericho and of the other inhabitants of the land. She had heard about the miracles God had performed for Israel—the parting of the Red Sea and the great victories over the Amorites on the other side of Jordan (vv. 9–11).

But there was a great difference between Rahab and the other Canaanites. She acted on what she knew. She acknowledged that God was the one true God. Her statement of faith was very specific when she said: "'For the LORD your God, He is God in heaven above and on earth beneath'" (v. 11).

Rahab's fellow Canaanites, who had the same knowledge as she, did not acknowledge the God of heaven. They would not respond to the light they had been given. And because of their unbelief, they were heading for immediate and eternal destruction and separation from God.

A Faith that Works

We've already seen how Rahab's faith was initially tested. We've also seen the way she passed the test. Her faith was real! But her greatest test lay ahead (vv. 12–21).

An Unselfish Request

If I had been Rahab, knowing that defeat and destruction was on its way, my first temptation would be to ask the spies if I could leave with them. Rather than telling them where to hide (v. 16), I'd have wanted to *show them* the hill country where we all could hide!

Rahab must have faced this temptation. This was her golden opportunity to join the children of Israel before doom and devastation hit Jericho. But she did not yield to those thoughts. She overcame temptation. If she wavered at all, it is not noticeable in the historical record, for her first request was not for herself but for her household (v. 12). "'Spare my father and my mother and my brothers and my sisters, with all who belong to them,'" she pleaded (v. 13).

The men of Israel responded by telling her to hang a "cord of scarlet thread" in her window and bring all of her relatives into her home. They assured her that when Israel marched on Jericho, she and all those in her home would be spared (v. 18).

The Stalks of Flax

Reflect for a moment on the "stalks of flax which Rahab had laid in order on the roof" of her home (v. 6). Gathering flax was a very tedious and laborious task. Industrious women of old would spend hours gathering these stalks to make cloth. In fact, the author of Proverbs describes a *virtuous* woman as one who "looks for wool and flax, and works with her hands in delight" (Prov. 31:13).

If Rahab had still been practicing her old profession, chances are she would not be gathering flax, since prostitutes are not known for the time they spend doing this kind of respectable work. Note, too, that Rahab had gathered enough flax to cover two grown men. Evidently she had been in the cloth business for a lengthy period of time.

The Scarlet Rope

The "scarlet rope" or "thread"—even more than the flax—points to a change of profession. When the ancients made dye, they would boil it out of rocks. And since liquid dye was difficult to transport and store, they would put a piece of rope into the dye to absorb it. Cloth makers then would buy pieces of the rope to dye their clothes. While the cloth was boiling in water, they would drop a piece of the dyed rope in the container and the color would transfer from the rope to the fabric. Usually a very small piece of rope—six inches or so—would dye a large quantity of cloth.

This is an important point. Rahab had enough red rope accumulated to hang it all the way over a wall that may have been as high as thirty feet. For a clothmaker, that's a lot of rope! Evidently Rahab's cloth business was no minor operation. She may have changed her profession years before.[1]

The House Left Standing

When the spies returned to the camp of Israel, they reported to Joshua that the Canaanites were very frightened. "'Surely,'" they said, "'the LORD has given all the land into our hands'" (2:24). But probably the most intriguing story they shared was their encounter with Rahab and how they had promised her deliverance when Israel attacked Jericho.

However, there was something the spies did not yet know. God was going to destroy the walls of Jericho—*and Rahab lived on the wall!* Can you imagine the consternation that must have gripped these men when God eventually revealed His battle plan to the children of Israel?

As we'll see in a future chapter, the walls of Jericho did fall down (6:20)! But, what happened to Rahab's house when this happened? There can be only one explanation! Standing, for all to see, was one small section of the wall with one lonely house—a house with a scarlet rope hanging from the window. Rahab and her entire family were saved. God honored her faith!

Becoming God's Man Today

Principles to Live By

What can all of us as men learn from a converted prostitute? Perhaps one of the greatest lessons is that we *can* learn from women—even a woman like Rahab. But there's more!

Principle 1. God is no respecter of persons.

One of the best ways to bridge the gap between this Old Testament story and our lives today is to look at a New Testament parallel. Many years later, the apostle John wrote that Jesus *"had* to pass through Samaria" (John 4:4). There is a sense of predetermined urgency in this statement, just as there was in Joshua's order to the spies when he said, "Go, view the land, especially Jericho." Furthermore, in both of these stories we encounter women of ill repute. Both responded to the light they had and both became witnesses of their faith.

The greatest lesson that jumps off the pages of Joshua chapter 2 and John chapter 4 is that God is no respecter of persons. Why else would He give so much space in the midst of divine history to record the conversion of two such people? God's desire is that all people know that Jesus Christ died for the sins of the world. There's no individual outside the sphere of His love and grace (John 3:16).

There's another intriguing fact in Scripture that indicates God's love for sinners. Since Rahab had become a believer, why then would God choose to record her name in the New Testament as "Rahab the harlot"? Why didn't He simply identify her as "Rahab the believer"? Was it not to demonstrate that He indeed is no respecter of persons and that all men and women everywhere can call on the name of the Lord and be saved (Rom. 10:13)?

This is not a new phenomenon in Scripture. One of the apostles was called Simon the Zealot (Mark 3:18). Zealots were radical Jews, similar to groups in our own culture who use violent tactics to bring about reform. Zealots were often involved with assault and killing. Obviously, Simon changed his profession after becoming a follower of Jesus Christ. And yet he retained his name—Simon the Zealot—evidence of God's grace in calling such a man to be one of His choicest servants.

Rahab, then, entered Israel with a name of shame. But she was a woman of faith! She was redeemed. Like Abraham, when Rahab believed God, He counted it to her as righteousness (Rom. 4:22). In fact, Rahab's name appears in the genealogy of Jesus Christ—the Savior of the world (Matt. 1:5).

Principle 2. True faith produces works.

Faith is an action word. James wrote, "Faith, if it has no works, is dead" (James 2:17). Rahab had an active faith. In that sense, she was "justified by works" (James 2:25). She was saved by faith (Rom. 5:1) but she proved her faith was real by her works. The quality of Rahab's faith stands out in at least four ways:

Taking God at His Word

Rahab's first words were, "I know" (Josh. 2:9). She believed that the God of Israel was the one true God and that He alone could be trusted.

What about you? How strong is your faith? Do you believe in God and in His Son Jesus Christ with the same intensity as Rahab? Remember, your light is much greater than hers, as was Israel's. Is your faith commensurate with your knowledge?

Taking a Stand

Rahab's faith produced self-denial. She refused to go along with the rest of the world. She gave up her former profession and became a clothmaker. In protecting God's messengers, she denied everything her countrymen stood for. With this act of faith she renounced everything in her past. She was no longer a part of sinful Jericho. Her life chnged, and people noticed it.

What about you? Does your faith in Jesus Christ really make a difference in the way you live? Are you willing to put your life and reputation on the line because of your commitment to God and to His system of values?

Showing Concern for Others

Rahab's faith resulted in concern for her whole family. She convinced them to come to her house and stay there for the seven days the army of Israel circled the city. She had no way of knowing when the attack was going to come, but she must have communicated as if the walls were going to fall at any moment. She operated with a sense of urgency.

What about you? Do you really believe that people are lost without Christ and that a final judgment is eventually coming? Obviously we can become neurotic and obsessed about this, not trusting God to carry out His divine and sovereign plan. But on the other hand, we must blend human responsibility with His divine perspective. God has given us the task to share His message of grace with those who do not know Him personally.

Simply Believing God

Rahab's theology was simple but her faith was great. She didn't know much, but what she knew determined her actions.

What about you? For some, knowledge gets in the way of faith. How unfortunate! The more we know about God, the more we should believe God. We must not get lost in a theological maze, trying to unravel all the ramifications of God's great plan and miss His greatest desire for us—that we simply trust in Him with all our hearts and act on that faith!

Points of Action

➤ Do you really believe God cares about your spiritual welfare? Do you believe He will forgive your sins no matter what you have done? If you have any doubts about this, think about Rahab! God does care about you! That's why He sent His only Son into this world to die for our sins. Receive Jesus Christ today as your Savior and Lord!

➤ As a Christian man, consider the following five areas in your life. Select one area that you feel is the weakest and needs the most attention. Decide on one specific way you can change that area of your life. For example, if you select number one, write out one area where you are not taking God at His word. Then pray and ask God to help you reach this goal.

1. I really take God at His Word.

2. I have taken a stand against those values that reflect "the lust of the flesh and the lust of the eyes and the boastful pride of life" (1 John 2:16).

3. I do not allow a fear of ridicule and persecution to affect my Christian lifestyle.

4. I am actively witnessing for Christ, believing that judgment is actually coming someday.

5. I'm simply believing God even though I don't understand all of the profound aspects of theology.

A Man's Man Is a Godly Man

Reread the questions under Points of Action. As you do, ask the Holy Spirit to impress on your heart one lesson you need to apply more effectively in your life. Then write out a specific goal. For example, you may be struggling to be true to biblical values. The world tends to press you into its mold. You know that you're not being consistent.

Set a Goal

With God's help, I will begin immediately to carry out the following goal in my life:

_____

_____

_____

_____

Memorize the Following Scripture

And without faith it is impossible to please Him, for he who comes to God must believe that He is, and that He is a rewarder of those who seek Him.
HEBREWS 11:6

Chapter 4

An Example of Faith and Humility
Read Joshua 3:1–17

*I*magine that your family is in desperate trouble. You are facing financial obstacles so gigantic there is no way you are going to survive economically. You may lose your home, your business, and your reputation. In fact, you are in such deep trouble that your greatest fear is that you might lose your family.

And then . . . God speaks to you directly—in an audible voice! He tells you that He is going to exalt you in the presence of your whole family. He is going to work a great miracle—and you will be the one to lead your family out of the deep crisis. God next reveals that as a result of delivering your family, everyone who sees the miracle happen will consider you a great hero.

God then says that you are to tell your family what He has just revealed to you. How would you react? Obviously, you would consider sharing everything God told you—including the statement that He was going to exalt *you!* After all, that *is* what God said. And you were supposed to tell your family what God said!

Now, multiply this fantasy a thousand times, substituting the name "Joshua" for yours and think in terms of "your family" being *all* the children of Israel. However, don't consider it a fantasy but a reality.

In this chapter we're going to see what Joshua did when confronted with an opportunity to exalt himself based on a direct message from God. His response is impressive.

When the Two Spies Returned!

When Joshua's two spies returned from Jericho, they were enthusiastic about entering the land of Canaan. From a human perspective, Joshua must have breathed a sigh of relief when he read their report—"Surely the LORD has given all the land into our hands, and all the inhabitants of the land, moreover, have melted away before us'" (Josh. 2:24).

A Confirmation

God had already reassured Joshua that the land was theirs (1:2–4). And Joshua believed what God had said (vv. 10–11). But the positive report from the two spies added a touch of reality that bolstered his faith. God knew what His servant needed. And though He had made it very clear that victory was already guaranteed if they met His conditions, the Lord allowed Joshua to accumulate some military evidence to make it easier to continue to actively believe God's promise and to communicate with confidence to the nation Israel.

A Raging River

Joshua's greatest test of faith, however, lay just ahead (3:1–6). Though the Canaanites who lived beyond Jordan appeared to be no obstacle, the children of Israel faced a raging river that separated them from the land. Spies or no spies, this problem was in many respects just as great as the one Moses faced when he stood on the shore of the Red Sea with no human means to get to the other side.

As we've seen from the story of Rahab, true faith and godly works go hand in hand. So it was in the life of Joshua! He wasted no time after he had received the positive report from his spies.

He broke camp "early in the morning" and moved the whole company of Israelites close to the Jordan River (see the map below).

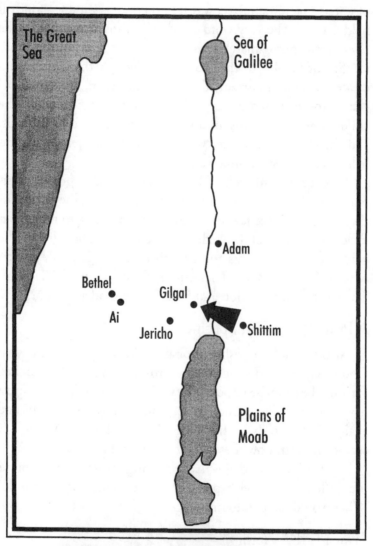

Crossing the Jordan

A New Generation

Can you imagine what was going through the minds of the children of Israel? Ahead of them was a wide and rushing torrent of water. The Jordan River was at flood tide, as wide as a football field is long. The very word "Jordan" means "descender." The river drops approximately one thousand feet in its journey from the Sea of Galilee to the Dead Sea. Though this descent has created a natural current, during flood season, the speed increases to nearly ten miles per hour. There was no way for the children of Israel to cross over with their children, their animals, and their supplies. There were no bridges, no ferryboats, no helicopters—just rushing water.

Most of the children of Israel who faced this present crisis represented a new generation. Most had not seen the parting of the Red Sea. Those few who had were too young to remember it clearly. Because of disobedience, their parents had died in the wilderness. Most of this new generation had heard only reports of what God had done. Their minds must have been filled with a mixture of anticipation and fear. Would God act again?

A Promise without Specifics

At this juncture, Joshua probably didn't know exactly what God was going to do to get them across the river. As he marched forward, bearing the responsibility of thousands of lives, he must have bolstered his courage by repeating to himself again and again God's words to him after Moses' death: "'Moses My servant is dead; now therefore arise, cross this Jordan'" (1:2).

On the human side Joshua was facing the greatest test of his life. What if nothing happened? What would the people do? What would happen to his image?

"Faith Is the Victory"

But Joshua's faith overruled his fears. Furthermore, his faith was contagious. The Levitical priests led the way carrying the

Ark of the Covenant, a small box, probably about four feet long, two and a half feet wide, and about two and a half feet high. It was overlaid with gold inside and out. The ark contained the tables of stone on which God Himself had written the law, as well as other symbols of God's leadership.

When the people set up camp, the ark was placed in the holy of holies in the Tabernacle (Exod. 26:33). Now it was being carried out ahead of Israel as they marched toward Jordan. And since the ark represented God's presence, the children of Israel sensed that God Himself was leading them right up to the edge of the river.

The depth of Joshua's faith is seen in his confident statement to the people: "'Consecrate yourselves, for tomorrow the LORD will do wonders among you'" (Josh. 3:5).

The specifics seemingly were yet to be revealed, but Joshua believed that God would give those instructions when they were needed. And because God is faithful to His promises, He did just that!

Another Message from God

Early in my Christian life, I was confused about the subject of faith. Somehow I thought that faith involved a leap in the dark. "If God says it, I believe it," I would often say.

Today I would still say, "If God says it, I believe it!" But there's a difference. I now know that I need not apologize or become defensive about faith in God's Word as it is revealed in the Bible. I now understand that God has never asked people to believe in something that is not based on reality and upon substantial facts. When God asked Joshua to approach the Jordan River and to believe that the waters would roll back (3:7–8), Joshua's faith was based not only on God's direct statements to him personally, but upon previous experience, which included the similar, very dramatic parting of the Red Sea.

God's Direct Communication

It's very important to note that Joshua's work of faith was not based on *blind* faith—some inner thoughts or intuitive feelings. It was faith based on fact. God spoke, not through some inner voice or existential experience, but through *direct revelation*. Joshua miraculously *heard* the voice of God say, "I'm going to take you across Jordan," just as God had verified His presence with Israel on many occasions when Moses was leading them.

Once again God was speaking directly to Joshua, and just at the right time. As they approached this raging torrent, God said, "'This day I will begin to exalt you in the sight of all Israel, that they may know that just as I have been with Moses, I will be with you'" (v. 7).

A Specific Promise—A Specific Meaning

When God said to Joshua, "'Just as I have been with Moses, I will be with you'" (1:5; 3:7), He was referring to that great event many years before when Israel was being pursued by the Egyptian army. The Red Sea lay ahead and their enemies were bearing down on them with lightning speed! It was then—not before—that God told Moses to stretch out his rod over the Red Sea. Megatons of water stood up in a heap and Israel passed over on *dry ground*. When they arrived safely on the other side, God instructed Moses to wave his rod over the sea again. The great mounds of water gave way and destroyed the Egyptian army.

As these memories flooded Joshua's mind, he understood clearly the meaning of this present promise. God's power was going to be with him as it was with Moses. He also understood the significance of God's specific instructions to the priests to walk into the waters of Jordan, carrying the ark. When they stood still, they would witness another dramatic miracle (3:8).

To understand what was happening, visualize what the Jordan River was like at flood tide. When conditions were normal, the river flowed at a much lower level. But when the snow began to melt in the mountains, the Jordan overflowed its banks to a second level which was ordinarily covered with shrubs and other growth. When the priests stepped into the water that day, the river was probably at its highest point (3:15).

God's Mouthpiece

The Bible does not record many times when God spoke directly to a large group of people. He usually spoke to one or a few individuals—people He had especially selected to be His divine mouthpiece. At this time in the history of Israel, Joshua was God's divine messenger to them (3:9–13).

A Man's Greatest Temptation

After God spoke directly to Joshua, notice what he said to the people: "Today you will begin to see God exalt *me* in your presence!"

Is this what Joshua said to the people? Not at all! It's what God said to Joshua, not what Joshua said to the children of Israel. Rather, Joshua said, "'By this you shall know that the *living God is among you!*'" (v. 10).

By rights, Joshua could have repeated exactly what God had said to him. But he didn't. There was no hint of pride or arrogance! His concern was that God be honored and glorified in what was about to happen.

But think of the temptation Joshua must have faced. How easy it would have been to draw attention to himself and to attempt to build his own ego. And what greater opportunity to engage in a lot of self-glorification. God Himself had spoken specifically to Joshua about the fact that He would exalt him.

A Man's Area of Greatest Vulnerability

Joshua, primarily because of his feelings of insecurity, was very vulnerable to this kind of temptation. Remember how threatened he was when he realized that Moses' mantle had fallen on his shoulders? He was so frightened he literally trembled. Fearful people are vulnerable to pride. They often overreact to praise and honor. Their temptation toward self-exaltation is often greater than it is in people who are basically secure.

Joshua, however, did not respond either with false humility or with pride. He had discovered security in God's promises to him. He was able to rise above the temptation to glorify himself. He gave honor to the only One who could be given credit for the miracle that was about to take place.

A Man God Could Trust

Joshua's response was admirable, especially in view of the fact that he had been fearful and threatened by this great task. But his response shows the main reason why God chose to use Joshua in the first place. He knew He could trust him with this leadership role. He knew Joshua could handle the temptation that comes to every individual who is entrusted with great responsibility.

Understand, however, that God *does use men*—their talents, their gifts, and their abilities. Joshua was a leader God could use. He had proven himself many times. He was a brilliant strategist. He had sent out the spies, he had thought through the issues, and he had communicated effectively to his leaders. But when it came to telling the children of Israel what God's plan was for him specifically, he completely bypassed the opportunity to exalt himself. What a mark of spiritual maturity!

Moving Out!

The great event was about to happen! In obedience—and by faith—the priests stepped into the river (3:14–17). The rushing waters stopped and began to back up—all the way to the city of Adam. What a sight this must have been! Some scholars believe the city of Adam was located as much as thirty miles up river (see the map on page 53).

What do you suppose the Canaanite spies were thinking when this unbelievable phenomenon happened? And what do you suppose happened to their morale when thousands of Israelites began to march across the Jordan on dry ground? Remember that this miracle could be *heard* and *seen* for miles around. In a matter of hours, every king on both sides of the Jordan was aware of what was happening.

With this miracle, God not only exalted Joshua in the eyes of the children of Israel. He also demonstrated once again His power and majesty to the pagan world, to lost mankind, to men and women and children He loved. He desired that they turn to Him in faith and obedience. He was giving the inhabitants of Canaan another opportunity to repent of their sins and turn from their gods of wood and stone to worship Him, the living and true God.

Personally I believe He would have saved every inhabitant in Canaan who would have turned to Him in faith—just as he did Rahab. To warn people of coming judgment and then to relent when people repent is part of the very character and nature of God.

A Rebellious Preacher

Take the Ninevites for instance. God charged Jonah to go and warn these people that He was going to destroy them because of their evil deeds. Jonah resisted. He went in the opposition direction, but eventually—after trying to avoid this responsibility—Jonah preached a message of doom in this great city. In forty days, Nineveh would be overthrown (Jon. 3:4). There were no "ifs or buts" in this message. Disaster was imminent.

But notice! The people of Nineveh listened to Jonah. They repented in sackcloth and ashes. And "when God saw their deeds, that they turned from their wicked way, then God relented concerning the calamity which He had declared He would bring upon them" (v. 10).

How Can This Be?

It may be difficult to understand how a sovereign God who declares something is going to happen can actually change His mind. But when people repent, God relents! Inherent in God's nature is the ability to withdraw His judgment when we return to Him.

You see, God had been issuing warning after warning to the Canaanites. Doom was on its way. From the Red Sea onward, with the miracles in the wilderness, with the forty years' judgment upon Israel, and now with the parting of the Jordan River, God was saying: Repent! Turn away from your wicked ways and your false gods and worship me! If you don't, judgment is coming.

And make no mistake about it! The Canaanites got the message. Remember what Rahab had reported to the spies?

> "We have heard how the LORD dried up the water of the Red Sea before you when you came out of Egypt, and what you did to the two kings of the Amorites who were beyond Jordan. . . . And when we heard it, our hearts melted and no courage remained in any man any longer because of you." (Josh. 2:10–11)

A Repentant Heart

Rahab had listened. She had turned from her sin and false gods to worship the one, true God: "'For the LORD your God,'" she testified, "'He is God in heaven above and on earth beneath'" (v. 11). But the vast majority of the Canaanites refused to give up their idolatry. Had they repented, had they listened to the voice of God through Israel, He would have turned away His wrath and with a heart of love welcomed them into the fold of security and protection. Jonah tells us this when he said:

> "For I knew that Thou art a gracious and compassionate God, slow to anger and abundant in lovingkindness, and one who relents concerning calamity." (Jon. 4:2)

Just so, this was God's message to the Canaanites as His people marched over Jordan.

Becoming God's Man Today

Principles to Live By

There are three dynamic lessons that emerge from this study.

Principle 1. God honors faith but He does not expect His children to operate on blind faith.

Frequently Bible teachers emphasize the importance of "faith" as they teach about many of these Old Testament characters. And, of course, it is true that faith is the focal point in many of their lives. This is very clear from Hebrews 11. But often we fail to emphasize that their faith was based squarely on facts—God's direct revelation and the promises He made to these faithful followers personally. This was true in Joshua's experience as he approached the Jordan River. He had great faith, but he also had great evidence and factual information on which to base that faith.

The "Experiential" Trap

Today many Christians are being led astray by relying on experience and feelings which are in some instances in direct opposition to the written Word of God. Experience—even what may appear to be *Christian* experience—can lead us into some very subtle traps. We must always make sure our feelings and desires (and faith) are in harmony with Scripture.

Proper Bible Interpretation

We also must make sure the promises we claim are promises for us today. For example, God never promised you or me that He would roll back the waters of the Jordan River, nor any river, for that matter. But because He had a special purpose in mind for Joshua and the children of Israel He performed this miracle for all to see—including the enemies of Israel.

On the other hand, God has promised us many things for our encouragement. For example, He promised that He would never leave us nor forsake us (Heb. 13:5; Matt. 28:20). His presence will always be with us. In other words, our responsibility as Christians is to base our faith on the direct teachings of Scriptures that are made to all believers of all time. This means that we must read our Bible carefully and prayerfully, seeking to know His will for us today.

"A Blind Leap!"

Another error that some Christians make is to give non-Christians the impression that Christian faith is a leap in the dark. Not so! Faith can and should be based on a reliable and trustworthy message. There is more internal and external evidence to trust the Bible and what it says than most other historical records. This statement may surprise some people, but it is factual. It is based on evidences that are well-known among those who have carefully compared the history in biblical documents with the history in other literature.[1]

A Personal Crisis of Faith

I became very disillusioned as a young Christian, primarily because I got my eyes off of God and on to human beings—three Christian leaders in particular who could not get along with each other. All confided in me regarding the others' weaknesses and "sins." Sadly, I couldn't handle this experience. I nearly "lost" my own faith.

In actuality, this "crisis of faith" turned out to be the most important one I had in my Christian experience. It caused me to evaluate much more carefully the basis of my faith. God graciously directed me to study under a great New Testament scholar, Dr. Merrill Tenney. God used this man to demonstrate that my faith could be based on a body of literature that was trustworthy and verifiable. He too had gone through a period of doubt, but in his search, discovered what he taught me—that the Bible is a book we can trust! Our faith in God and His Son Jesus Christ is not a "leap in the dark."

Principle 2. God honors Christians who honor Him.

Perhaps the most striking lesson to come out of this Old Testament story is the way in which Joshua gave glory to God. It would have been so easy for him to honor himself when God told Joshua directly that He was going to honor him that day.

This was one of Joshua's secrets to success as an Old Testament believer. And it is one of the secrets to successful Christian living. We must develop a proper balance and perspective on God's sovereign use of human beings. God does use our talents and our abilities. He actually wants us to have confidence in ourselves. He wants us to honor one another. But above all this, He wants the glory. He alone is God! He has made us! Without Him we can do nothing! Our very life and breath are in His hands.

The "Self-image" Trap

Your own temptation toward pride may be accentuated because of feelings of insecurity and a lack of self-worth. This sounds strange, but it's true! Often people with a self-image problem react to success like a dry sponge responds to water. Their need for positive feedback is so great that they overreact.

Whatever the cause of persistent pride and self-glorification, it is inappropriate behavior. We need to deal with the problem, forsake pride and honor and glorify God in all we do.

This does not mean that we should not accept honor and praise, but rather it means that we should develop the ability to handle them with balance and perspective. And the more we become secure within ourselves and in our Lord, the more we will be able to praise and honor God and others with naturalness and balance.

Principle 3. God is still reaching out to lost humanity.

One of God's primary purposes in calling Israel to be His special people was to use them as a nation to communicate His righteousness and love to a lost world. Today God's plan is to use His body, the church, to communicate this truth to those who do not know Him. Thus, He prayed to His Father before returning to heaven:

> "I do not ask in behalf of these alone [His disciples], but for those also who believe in Me through their word [all Christians of all time]; that they may all be one; . . . I in them, and Thou in Me, that they may be perfected in unity, *that the world may know that Thou didst send Me*, and didst love them, even as Thou didst love Me." (John 17:20–21, 23)

Peter also wrote regarding God's purpose in reaching the world:

> But you are a chosen race, a royal priesthood, a holy nation, a people for God's own possession, that you may proclaim the excellencies of Him who has called you out of darkness into His marvelous light; for you once were not a people, but now you are the people of God; you had not received mercy, but now you have received mercy.
>
> Beloved, I urge you as aliens and strangers to abstain from fleshly lusts, which wage war against the soul.
>
> Keep your behavior excellent among the Gentiles, so that in the thing in which they slander you as evildoers, they may on account of your good deeds, as they observe them, glorify God in the day of visitation. (1 Pet. 2:9–12)

Points of Action

The following questions will enable you to apply these lessons to your life personally. Zero in on the question that is most appropriate to your own spiritual need and decide today what you can do to be more effective as a Christian in that area of your life.

➤ To what extent am I trusting God based on a thorough knowledge of His Word and how it applies to me today?
___ never ___ a little ___ some ___ much

➤ To what extent am I giving glory and honor to God for what He has given me?
___ never ___ a little ___ some ___ much

➤ To what extent am I contributing to the effectiveness of Christ's body, the church, in order to provide a corporate image of love, unity and righteousness to the unsaved world?
___ never ___ a little ___ some ___ much

A Man's Man Is a Godly Man

Reread the above questions and the way in which you responded to the checklist. Ask the Holy Spirit to impress on your heart one lesson you need to apply more effectively in your life. Then write a specific goal. For example, you may have checked "a little" when it comes to giving glory and honor to God. You know this is a weakness in your life. You tend to take credit for yourself.

Set a Goal

With God's help, I will begin immediately to carry out the following goal in my life:

_____

_____

_____

_____

Memorize the Following Scripture

> *I, therefore, the prisoner of the Lord, entreat you to walk in a manner worthy of the calling with which you have been called, with all humility and gentleness, with patience, showing forbearance to one another in love, being diligent to preserve the unity of the Spirit in the bond of peace.*
>
> EPHESIANS 4:1–3

Chapter 5

A Cure for Fading Memories
Read Joshua 4:1–24

Watch yourself lest you forget. . . ." (Deut. 6:12). This was the warning Moses issued to all Israel just before they entered the Promised Land. And this is the warning God wants us to hear today!

How quickly our memories fade! How quickly we forget. This is particularly true when everything seems to be going our way.

Moses also spelled out for Israel *what* we forget—and why! More accurately, the "what" is "who"—God Himself. "Watch yourself lest you forget *the LORD*" (Deut. 6:12). And even more specifically, Moses warned Israel to remember that it was "the LORD" who brought them out of Egypt.

> It was the Lord who would bring them into a land flowing with milk and honey.

> It was the Lord who would make them victorious over their enemies.

> It was the Lord who would provide them with herds and flocks and silver and gold.

As is often the case with us, the children of Israel's temptation would be to become proud and to say—"We did this ourselves!" (read Deut. 6–8).

Memorial Stones

God taught the children of Israel many important truths on their journey from Egypt to Canaan, but none more important than the lesson surrounding the "memorial stones" (Josh. 4:1–5, 9–20). Whether or not they took this lesson to heart would, in many respects, determine their destiny as a nation.

God had just worked another great miracle for Israel. The raging waters of the Jordan River rose "up in one heap . . . while all Israel crossed on dry ground" (3:16–17). Miraculously, when the priests stepped into the river carrying the Ark of the Covenant, the rushing waters were suddenly cut off.

Over forty years earlier, when the children of Israel had crossed the Red Sea, they had left the land of bondage (Egypt). Now, as they crossed over the Jordan, they were entering a land that promised to be a place of freedom (Canaan).

For them to enjoy this freedom, however, they were required to live up to some very specific conditions which had been outlined by God. They must never forget the commandments He gave them at Mt. Sinai—and they must obey these commandments. God's instructions regarding the "memorial stones" in Joshua 4 serve as a way to help Israel remember.

"Trust Me with All Your Hearts"

Before the priests ever stepped foot into the Jordan River, God had given Joshua some general instructions regarding what should happen once they crossed the river. Twelve men were selected, one from each tribe, to carry out the rest of God's plan as soon as the children of Israel crossed over Jordan (3:12).

This is the way God often works! He doesn't reveal all of His will at one time. But as we respond to the light we have, He adds more light and clears the path ahead of us. Our responsibility is to trust Him—with all our hearts and to avoid leaning on our own understanding. And if we acknowledge Him in all our ways, then, God "will make your paths straight" (Prov. 3:5–6).

This is exactly what happened to the children of Israel. Once they "had finished crossing," the Lord gave more specific instructions. These twelve men were to go back to the center of the riverbed where the priests were still standing, holding the ark. Each man was to pick up a large rock or stone from the "middle of the Jordan" and carry it to the side of the river where Israel now camped in the land of Canaan (Josh. 4:3–5).

"Go Where?"

Imagine what these twelve men must have thought, *Go back into the middle of the Jordan?* Israel must have taken most of the day to complete the crossing. And the waters were still piled high, the ground still dry! But how long would it last?

Whatever their feelings and anxiety, these men obeyed. They did not allow whatever fear they may have felt to dominate and control them. By faith they reentered the riverbed. We read that they "took up twelve stones from the middle of the Jordan, just as the LORD spoke to Joshua, according to the number of the tribes of the sons of Israel; and they carried them over with them to the lodging place and put them down there" (v. 8).

"I'll Go with You"

I'm convinced there's another reason why these men obeyed God so quickly. Joshua not only issued God's order, but he personally joined these men on their rather strange mission back into the riverbed. Should the Jordan suddenly return to normal, it would have taken not only the lives of the twelve men and the priests—who still faithfully stood in the middle of the river holding the ark—but Joshua's life as well. Together—with their leader—these men courageously tackled this task.

Another Pile of Stones

Something very interesting happened once they arrived in the middle of the Jordan. While the twelve men were transporting their stones back to the shore, Joshua—in his excitement—suddenly began to pile up stones in the middle of the river, right at the feet of the priests.

There is no record that God had instructed him to do this. It appears to be a spontaneous act of worship. Joshua already knew what God's purpose was in having them carry the stones *from Jordan*, so he simply decided to pile up twelve stones *in Jordan* as a personal testimony to what God had done for Israel in backing up the waters of the Jordan River. The text tells us that these stones "are there to this day" (v. 9).

That does not mean the stones are still stacked in the middle of the Jordan River to our "present day." If you look, you won't find them. Rather, at the time Joshua recorded the event, the stones still stood as a tribute to God's great power. When the waters subsided, they would become visible. And as the waters rose and fell over the next several years, the stones would stand as a memorial to God's love and care for Israel.

Why Twelve Stones?

Once these twelve men had carried the twelve stones to the shore of Canaan, and after Joshua built an altar in the middle of the river with twelve more stones, he commanded the priests to finish crossing the river with the Ark of the Covenant. The moment their feet touched the other side, the wall of water that had piled up for miles back up the river came crashing forward. We read, "The waters of the Jordan returned to their place, and went over all its banks as before" (4:18).

What an awe-inspiring sight this must have been for the children of Israel as they stood in the land of Canaan watching the completion of this great miracle. But following their shouts of joy and triumph there must have been a gradual silence that crept over them. Everything seemed so normal again. The water was rushing and swirling down to the Dead Sea as it had before. For some the whole experience may have been like a dream. Did this really happen? That very morning they had stood on one side of the mighty rushing Jordan. Now they were on the other side. How could it be?

On to Gilgal

The children of Israel moved on to Gilgal (see map on p. 53) carrying the twelve stones from the Jordan, proof that the experience was no dream. It was a reality. And there in Gilgal the stones were set up as a memorial (v. 20).

God stated the purpose for these stones at the same time He instructed Joshua to have the twelve men from each tribe transport them from the middle of the river. And Joshua shared this purpose with these men prior to their involvement in the project (vv. 6–7). But the most complete statement of purpose is found at the end of this chapter when Joshua spoke to all the people of Israel as the stones were being set up in Gilgal.

> "When your children ask their fathers in time to come, saying, 'What are these stones?' then you shall inform your children, saying, 'Israel crossed this Jordan on dry ground.' For the LORD your God dried up the waters of the Jordan before you until you had crossed, just as the LORD your God had done to the Red Sea, which He dried up before us until we had crossed." (vv. 21–23)

This was God's primary reason. These stones were to remind Israel and succeeding generations that God is a God of great power and glory and it was He who brought them over Jordan. They were also to be a witness to unbelievers. Thus, God stated that these stones were set up so "that all the peoples of the earth may know that the hand of the LORD is mighty" (v. 24).

Once again we see God's great concern for all mankind. One of His primary purposes in choosing Israel and loving them as His own chosen people was to use them as a dramatic means to communicate to lost humanity that He is a God who cares about their eternal destiny. And the message *was* heard! It went throughout the whole land! In Joshua 5:1, we read:

Now it came about when all the kings of the Amorites who were beyond the Jordan to the west, and all the kings of the Canaanites who were by the sea, heard how the LORD had dried up the waters of the Jordan before the sons of Israel until they had crossed, that their hearts melted, and there was no spirit in them any longer, because of the sons of Israel.

What Happened?

Hardened Hearts

How wonderful it would be if we could report that the Canaanites, upon seeing and hearing about this great demonstration of God's power and loving concern for Israel, repented of their sins, turned from their wicked ways and joined Rahab in following the one true God. But they didn't. Like Pharaoh in Egypt, their fears soon turned to pride and arrogance. They hardened their hearts against God and refused to acknowledge who He really is! How tragic!

Fading Memories

But even more tragic, God's own chosen people, Israel, failed to remind their children of what God had done. No sooner had they settled into the land flowing with milk and honey than their memories began to fade. Even the memorial stones were forgotten by the majority in Israel.

One of the most heartbreaking and sobering statements in all of Scripture is recorded in Judges 2. At this moment, many years had passed since Israel crossed over Jordan and set up the memorial stones in Gilgal. God had given them victory after victory. After years of bondage and wilderness wanderings, they settled into the land and enjoyed the freedom of having a place to live in peace and plenty. But something was happening to the children of Israel, something that is almost unbelievable. We read:

Then Joshua the son of Nun, the servant of the LORD, died at the age of one hundred and ten . . . and all that generation also were gathered to their fathers; and there arose another generation after them who did not know the LORD, nor yet the work which He had done for Israel. (Judg. 2:8, 10)

How Could This Be?

How could a people who had witnessed such incredible miracles ever forget them? The facts are, they did. The parents in Israel failed to tell their children what God had done for them at Jordan and how He continued to give them victories over their enemies. Consequently, their children turned away from God and "did evil" and "served the Baals" in Canaan. The biblical record speaks for itself:

They forsook the LORD, the God of their fathers, who had brought them out of the land of Egypt, and followed other gods from among the gods of the peoples who were around them, and bowed themselves down to them; thus they provoked the LORD to anger. (v. 12)

Sadly—and incredibly—in just two generations, all of Israel had forsaken the God who was responsible for everything they had.

Becoming God's Man Today

A Principle to Live By

Principle 1. When we fail to model and teach God's Word, it only takes one generation for degeneration to take place.

America Is Exhibit "A"

It may be difficult to comprehend how such a change could take place in Israel in such a short period of time. But think for a moment about what has happened in American culture in the last fifty to sixty years. Our whole value system has changed, which has affected the family unit dramatically. When we ceased to reflect God's values in our homes, it only took one generation for spiritual degeneration to take place.

When as parents we fail to teach our children respect and love for God and His Word by both word and example—when we fail to communicate to them who He is—we are on the road to spiritual disaster. As society has changed, so has the family. And as the family has changed, it has increased the changes in society. The changes that took place in Israel are no different than the changes that are taking place in America.

If we go back to the beginning of our American culture, it is easy to detect that our society reflected a biblical value system in our marital and family life, in our business ethics, in our recreational and entertainment activities, in our academic institutions and in government. Biblical precepts and principles were

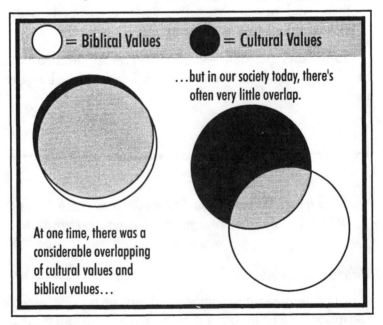

= Biblical Values = Cultural Values

...but in our society today, there's often very little overlap.

At one time, there was a considerable overlapping of cultural values and biblical values...

a part of the fabric of our society. We were a nation built upon the value system that grew out of the Hebrew-Christian ethic as spelled out in the Bible. Our civil laws were forged out of the teachings of Scripture.

Conflicting Values

In two generations, our nation has changed (see the illustration on the preceeding page). In some respects, there is very little overlap between what the Bible says is right and wrong and what our culture accepts as right and wrong. In many cases, we still verbalize the old values, but we do not abide by them in our daily lives. We have moved from believing in a system of absolutes to a completely relativistic approach in making decisions in the area of personal and social ethics.

The "Frog in the Kettle"

Unfortunately, even Christian families—people who profess to believe the Bible—are being seriously influenced and affected by our changing value system. They are finding it difficult to be in the world without being a part of the world (John 17:14–16). The fact is, our thinking has become confused and out of focus. The impact of the media (television, movies, literature), and particularly of our educational institution, has little by little influenced our thinking in ways we are not even aware.

George Barna calls this the "frog in the kettle" syndrome. As the water heats up, it gradually overpowers the frog who is not aware of the change in temperature. Thus, we too have been overpowered by the value changes that have gradually taken place in our society.

This Was Israel's Problem!

God warned the children of Israel very early in their journey from Egypt to Canaan not to allow the environment they were going into to cause them to fail to acknowledge Him and to teach their children who He was and what He had done for them. God said through Moses:

> "Watch yourself, *lest you forget* the LORD who brought you from the land of Egypt, out of the house of slavery. You shall fear only the LORD your God; and you shall worship Him, and swear by His name. You shall not follow other gods, any of the gods of the peoples who surround you, for the LORD your God in the midst of you is a jealous God; otherwise the anger of the LORD your God will be kindled against you, and He will wipe you off the face of the earth." (Deut. 6:12–15)

Read and Compare

Later Moses made the warning even more specific, spelling out some of the things that could cause the Israelites to forget the Lord. As you read, compare it to what has happened in American society:

> "For the LORD your God is bringing you into a good land, a land of brooks of water, of fountains and springs, flowing forth in valleys and hills; a land of wheat and barley, of vines and fig trees and pomegranates, a land of olive oil and honey; a land where you shall eat food without scarcity, in which you shall not lack anything; a land whose stones are iron, and out of whose hills you can dig copper. When you have eaten and are satisfied, you shall bless the LORD your God for the good land which He has given you. Beware lest you forget the LORD your God by not keeping His commandments and His ordinances and His statutes which I am commanding you today; lest, when you have eaten and are satisfied, and have built good houses and lived in them, and when your herds and your flocks multiply, and your silver and gold multiply, and all that you have multiplies then your heart becomes proud, and you forget the LORD your God who brought you out from the land of Egypt, out of the house of slavery." (8:7–14)

Israel Even Forgot the Memorial Stones

Unfortunately, Israel forgot the warnings of Moses. And when the new generation that was eventually allowed to enter Canaan was reminded of these truths with the memorial stones, they even forgot to use these stones as God intended. They failed to teach their children about the One who brought them over Jordan.

So one generation later, the nation was involved in unbelievable materialism, hideous idolatry and the worst sorts of immorality. Consequently, God's hand of judgment fell on them and they were eventually scattered to the ends of the earth.

Principle 2. The Bible teaches that as men we have a tremendous responsibility to take the lead in teaching our children biblical values.

What is happening in your home and mine? What will our children remember about us? Will they remember a beautiful home, big-screen television, video players, computer games, fast cars, a vacation home, a speedboat, an open-ended allowance—and all the frantic efforts we put forth to accumulate and keep these possessions?

Don't misunderstand! God does not say that material things are wrong and out of the will of God. If they were, God wouldn't have given the children of Israel all the things mentioned in Deuteronomy 6 and 8. Both Abraham and Job would be millionaires by today's standards (Job 42:10–12).

Material things, therefore, are not the issue. Our attitude toward them—and God—is! The children of Israel became materialists. They took the credit for their blessings. Eventually they turned away from God to false gods—the gods of a pagan society. And, in the process, they failed to teach their children their sacred history.

What about us? Do we even have any memorial stones that can remind us and our children about God's blessings?

I had the privilege of being reared in a Christian family. My parents were quite involved in a kind of Christianity that was rather legalistic, and they were somewhat theologically confused, there was a reality about their lives I shall never forget. They never forced me or my brothers and sisters to accept their faith or their standards of conduct, but they consistently loved us, provided for us, and demonstrated their trust and faith in God. And they never hesitated to teach us what God said in the Bible.

Though cultural values have changed drastically since my childhood and adolescent years, I still believe in the values I was taught as a child. True, I refined my convictions in the light of the teachings of Scripture, but my heritage still stands. I thank God for my Christian parents.

Unfortunately, not everyone has the benefit of God-honoring parents. Parents today, just as parents in Joshua's day, fail to obey God in this respect. But, we need not fail—just as Israel was not destined to failure. And if we do fail, it is never too late to begin doing something about it—even if the only thing we can do is ask forgiveness.

Points of Action

Answer the following questions as honestly as possible. Write out one thing you can do immediately to help your children sense the reality of God.

> What "memorial stones" are there in my home—and in my personal life—that demonstrate that God exists and that we are dependent upon Him for life and existence?

> In what ways do we talk about God? Is He a living reality or just a theological idea?

> In what ways can I convey to my children a reverence and respect for God? In what ways can I convey to my children that everything we have comes from Him?

A Man's Man Is a Godly Man

Reread the questions under Points of Action. As you do, ask the Holy Spirit to impress on your heart one lesson you need to apply more effectively in your life. Then write out a specific goal. For example, as a father, you would like to do more to convey to your children reverence and respect for God. To do this, you know you need to develop this quality in your own life.

Set a Goal

With God's help, I will begin immediately to carry out the following goal in my life:

_____

_____

_____

Memorize the Following Scripture

"And these words, which I am commanding you today, shall be on your heart; and you shall teach them diligently to your sons and shall talk of them when you sit in your house and when you walk by the way and when you lie down and when you rise up. And you shall bind them as a sign on your hand and they shall be as frontals on your forehead. And you shall write them on the doorposts of your house and on your gates."
DEUTERONOMY 6:6–9

Chapter 6

Remembrances: More Than Rituals!
Read Joshua 5:1–15

*O*ne of the most exciting experiences in my life as a Christian was in the Ukraine shortly after Mikhail Gorbachev led the Soviet Union into the era of *perestroika*. I participated in a baptismal service on a public beach. Only a few months earlier, what took place would have been unheard of. Nearby, listening and watching, were a number of people who claimed to be communistic and atheistic. This experience was so unusual because for nearly seventy years it was illegal to openly practice Christianity in this country that was committed to atheistic materialism. But *glasnost* (open expression of varying points of view) and *perestroika* (social restructuring) changed all that!

I had always believed and taught that a major purpose of baptism was to publicly proclaim the message of Christ's death and resurrection and the new life we can have in Christ. But this time, I had the opportunity to worship God in a setting that had been pagan for so long. What a thrill it was to set the stage for the baptisms by preaching a message from the Word of God.

Why These Public Symbols?

God knows how easily we forget! This is one reason why He instructed Joshua to remove twelve stones from the middle of the Jordan River and stack them up at Gilgal. They were to be a *memorial* to God's great power in bringing the nation of Israel into the Promised Land. They were to be a *means* of communicating to their children that God had "dried up the waters of the Jordan" just as He "had done to the Red Sea."

God also had another purpose for the memorial stones—to enable Israel to demonstrate before "all the peoples of the earth . . . that the hand of the LORD is mighty" and that Israel and all mankind "may fear the LORD" (4:24).

When God commanded Joshua to remember His acts of love and grace with additional symbols, it was not something new in Israel's history. And as we'll see, God continued to provide remembrances for His children even in New Testament days. Our memories are terribly short, and God has factored that into His great plan.

For Men Only

When this new generation of Israelites entered the land of Canaan, the Lord instructed Joshua to make sure all the sons of Israel were circumcised (5:2). God stated the reason for this command very clearly:

> And this is the reason why Joshua circumcised them: all the people who came out of Egypt who were males, all the men of war, died in the wilderness along the way, after they came out of Egypt. For all the people who came out were circumcised, but all the people who were born in the wilderness along the way as they came out of Egypt had not been circumcised. (vv. 4–5)

Father Abraham

God established circumcision as a special rite when He first called Abraham out of paganism and covenanted with him that He would bless this man with a *land,* a *seed,* and a *blessing* (Gen. 12:1–3). The "land" was Canaan! The "seed" was the nation Israel! And the "blessing" was the Savior who would come into the world to die for the sins of all mankind!

God confirmed that covenant with Abraham by means of circumcision. It was a "sign of the covenant" (17:9–14). Furthermore, it was to be a continual practice in Israel to remind God's people of His promises. Thus, God said to Abraham, "'Every male among you who is eight days old shall be circumcised *throughout your generations*'" (v. 12).

Why Circumcision?

We must realize first of all, that God's ways are very often not our ways. He does things that are sometimes difficult for our finite minds to grasp. Where our reasoning ends, His begins (Isa. 55:8–9; Rom. 11:33).

On the other hand, most of the things that God does and the demands He makes of His people make sense, particularly if we stop for a moment and think about it historically, culturally and scientifically. Whenever God acts, He usually achieves more than one purpose with the same event or situation.

Avoiding Cancer

About four thousand years after God's command to Abraham regarding circumcision, medical science discovered that wives of men who had not been circumcised have a greater incidence of cancer of the cervix than do wives of men who have been circumcised. This is particularly true in primitive cultures where personal cleanliness is an environmental problem. Putting it plainly and simply, circumcision promotes personal hygiene and helps eliminate virulent bacteria, including the "cancer-producing Smegma bacillus."[1]

In God's scheme of things, then, circumcision not only had spiritual significance but healthful benefits. Part of His promise to Abraham was a seed—multitudes of children and grandchildren for generations to come. With this promise of multiplication, God also selected the rite of circumcision as a means of personal protection from one of the most serious causes of death—cancer. It's interesting that even with all of our scientific knowledge, we have not to this day discovered a satisfactory cure for this deadly disease. However, God provided a way thousands of years ago to avoid it.

A Safe Procedure

Another interesting medical sidelight is that God commanded the parents of Israel to circumcise their male children on the *eighth day* following their birth (Gen. 17:12). Again, medical science has discovered that this is the best time in a child's life to perform this minor operation. Natural resources in the human body for preventing excessive bleeding reach a 110 percent level about the eighth day and then level off quickly following this point in time. Furthermore, before the eighth day, these natural resources have not yet been produced in sufficient quantity in the child's body to make the operation generally safe.[2] Once again we see God's wisdom in prescribing this specific rite as a sign of His covenant with Israel.

Spiritual Benefits

Scientific explanations for this symbolic act, as helpful as they are, are only secondary purposes. God's primary reasons for circumcision were spiritual.

First, no male child in Israel could miss this constant reminder that he was different from other male children who were not Israelites. There were many natural opportunities in these primitive cultures for parents to explain to both male and female children—and adults—why little boys were circumcised. The rite served as a constant reminder to Israel and the pagans around them of God's covenant with His chosen people. Not only did people observe the process, but they saw the results. When circumcised, a male in Israel was never the same again—even into adulthood.

Second—and related to the first—no male would ever be able to forget God's covenant. Even natural body functions served as a reminder.

Third, no wife in Israel would ever be able to forget God's covenant. With every intimate relationship with her husband, she was reminded that God had made a promise to them. Perhaps they even dreamed that they might be the parents of the Messiah, the promised seed.

Fourth, no man in Israel would ever be able to engage in illicit sexual activities with a pagan woman without being confronted with the fact that he was different from other males—a definite reminder of his chosen position in God's eternal plan. Even an act of sin would bring to his remembrance God's covenant.

In summary, when measured by scientific, cultural, historical, and spiritual criteria, there is no rite that God could have chosen to achieve His divine purposes through Israel more adequately than circumcision. This rite also demonstrates God's view of natural processes—from elimination to legitimate sexual relationships. Mankind perverts and makes unclean what God has created to be very natural and necessary. In fact, it is so natural and meaningful to God that He chose circumcision as a spiritual reminder of His own *personal relationship* with His people.

Overcoming the Reproach of Egypt

When the children of Israel entered Canaan after crossing the Jordan, God once again reminded them of His covenant. And to help them remember that covenant, He instructed them to once again circumcise all the males in Israel. With this act God also removed the "reproach of Egypt" from them (Josh. 5:9). The Egyptians had scoffed at the Israelites, suggesting that God had delivered them from their land in order to "kill them in the mountains" (Exod. 32:12). On this day, "When they had finished circumcising all the nation," they were delivered from that accusation. "'Today,'" the Lord said to Joshua, "'I have rolled away the reproach of Egypt from you'" (Josh. 5:9). They were indeed God's chosen people and He would never renege on His promise to Abraham—and to them. It was *unconditional, literal,* and *eternal.*

Food—A Universal Symbol

The Passover Meal

While the children of Israel were still in Egyptian bondage, God instituted another remembrance of His love and grace. It was the Passover meal connected with Israel's deliverance from slavery. After sending nine plagues on Egypt, God revealed that He was going to bring one final catastrophe. He was going to slay all the first-born, "from the first-born of the Pharaoh who sits on his throne, even to the first-born of the slave girl who is behind the millstones; all the first-born of the cattle as well" (Exod. 11:5). However, the children of Israel would be spared from this judgment if they sprinkled the blood of a lamb or goat on the doorposts of their houses. "'When I see the blood,'" the Lord promised, "'I will *pass over* you, and no plague will befall you to destroy you when I strike the land of Egypt'" (12:13).

A Regular Remembrance

And so it happened! Judgment fell, and all of Israel who had prepared themselves according to God's instructions were spared. It was very clear that God intended for Israel to remember the Lord's mercy perpetually by practicing the Passover. Thus we read: "'Now this day will be a *memorial* to you, and you shall celebrate it as a feast to the Lord; throughout your generations you are to celebrate it as a *permanent ordinance*'" (v. 14). To this day, devout Jews remember their deliverance from Egypt by engaging in the Passover and the Feast of Unleavened Bread.[3]

The Third Time Was Now!

As far as we can tell from Scripture, the Passover was observed only twice before the events in Joshua 5:10–12. The first time was on the evening before the Israelites left Egypt. The second time was in the wilderness of Sinai, a year after they left the land of bondage (Num. 9:1–5). And the third time was *now*—after the children of Israel wandered in the wilderness for forty years and a new generation entered Canaan. The celebration followed their experience in setting up the memorial stones and reinstating the rite of circumcision.

No More Manna!

To add to the drama of this occasion, once they had participated in the Passover meal, the manna that God had provided regularly—even when they were being judged for their sins as they wandered in the wilderness—ceased. For the first time, the children of Israel were able to eat "some of the yield of the land of Canaan," a direct fulfillment of God's promise to them many years before (Exod. 13:35; Josh. 5:12).

God's Purposes Are Clear

It's apparent what God had in mind with these remembrances. He was concerned that the children of Israel never forget all the things He had done for them.

The *memorial stones* would remind them and their children of His great power in parting the waters of the Red Sea and backing up the Jordan River. In their minds, it would also take them back in time to the Red Sea experience when they left Egypt.

Circumcision would help them remember God's unconditional covenant which He first gave to Abraham. They would be constantly reminded of God's great purpose in choosing them—to be a blessing to the whole world.

The *Passover* would remind them of His love and grace in sparing them from the horrible plague in Egypt. More importantly, this meal would remind them of the coming Messiah—the perfect Passover Lamb—who would shed His blood for the sins of the world.

But let us not forget God's dual purposes with all of these symbols. Not only were they to serve as remembrances and reminders to the children of Israel, but they were also to demonstrate God's love and grace to their pagan neighbors. With these visual demonstrations, God was reaching out to a lost and dying world.

Standing on Holy Ground

The grand culmination for all of these events involved a very personal experience for Joshua (5:13–15)—an experience that was reminiscent of Moses' experience when God spoke to him from a burning bush as he was "pasturing the flock of Jethro his father-in-law" (Exod. 3:1). On the backside of the desert, an angel of the Lord called to Moses out of the middle of the bush and told him to remove his sandals from his feet, for, said the angel, "'The place on which you are standing is holy ground'" (v. 5).

Joshua's experience following the Passover was similar. While he was preparing to attack Jericho, an armed man with a sword suddenly appeared to him. This stranger identified himself as "captain of the host of the Lord." Joshua immediately recognized God's presence in this man and he "fell on his face" and worshiped Him (Josh. 5:13–14). Unknown to Joshua at the time, this was probably an Old Testament appearance of every Christian's commander-in-chief, the Lord Jesus Christ.

The most significant similarity to that of Moses is that God was revealing to Joshua that the ground where he was standing at that moment was indeed holy because of God's awesome presence. Furthermore, God was no doubt communicating to

Joshua that the *entire land*—the land of Canaan—was also holy. God had set it apart for them and He wanted them to have it as their very own. God's will, of course, was that His people Israel would use that land as a means to reflect His holiness to all the peoples of the earth. Their lives were to reflect God's righteousness.

Becoming God's Man Today

Principles to Live By

Principle 1. Like Israel, we too need "remembrances" lest we forget what God has done for us.

Just as God instituted memorial events in the Old Testament, so He has instituted some very unique memorial events in the New Testament, which, as Christians, we are to practice to this very day.

Baptism

Baptism visualizes that we have died with Christ and have been resurrected to a new life. When people were converted to Jesus Christ in the first century, they were baptized. Thus Luke recorded—"So then, those who had received his [Peter's] word *were baptized*" (Acts 2:41a).

The Great Commission. Practicing baptism was a fulfillment of the Lord's will, for He had instructed His followers to "'go therefore and make disciples of all the nations, *baptizing them* in the name of the Father and the Son and the Holy Spirit'" (Matt. 28:19).

A Powerful Symbol. Baptism, like circumcision in the Old Testament, is a unique symbol—a sign. It is not a means of salvation which results from faith and faith only (Rom. 5:1; Eph. 2:8–9). Rather, baptism is a symbolic representation of Christ's death and resurrection.

For Believers Only. I believe that the New Testament teaches that baptism is for believers only—people who are old enough to make an intelligent decision for Jesus Christ. I also believe that the New Testament form for baptism is immersion, though I realize that some well-respected Christian scholars disagree on the mode.

Identification with Christ. The main purpose of baptism, however, is very clear. It's to remind all of us as Christians of our identification with Christ. But it's also to be a witness to unbelievers, communicating to them that Jesus died and rose again and that by faith in Him they can be buried with Him and raised to a new life. Every Christian who wants to be completely obedient to Jesus Christ should be baptized.

The Lord's Supper

The second memorial event is often called communion. When Jesus was eating the Passover meal with the apostles just before His death on the cross, He extended the significance of this religious meal into the life of the body of Christ, the church. As He broke the bread that evening with His followers and drank the cup with them, He demonstrated how His body would be bruised and His blood shed for the sins of the world. "Do this," He said, *"in remembrance of Me"* (Luke 22:19). Paul elaborated on Christ's words in his letter to the Corinthians when he wrote, "For as often as you eat this bread and drink the cup, you proclaim the Lord's death until He comes" (1 Cor. 11:26).

A Creative Experience. Down through church history, Christians have remembered the Lord with this ordinance. It has taken many forms—from a full meal to a token meal. But the form is not really that important. The meaning is! The communion experience is a remembrance—a remembrance of Christ's death for each of us.

The Cleansing Blood. Like Israel, we need a constant reminder that when God sees the blood—in this instance the blood of

Christ—He will pass over us in judgment. By the blood of the perfect Lamb of God, His Son Jesus Christ, we have been cleansed from our sins and set free from eternal judgment and death. As Paul wrote—"In Him [Christ] we have redemption through His blood, the forgiveness of our trespasses, according to the riches of His grace" (Eph. 1:7).

The House Church. The "bread" and the "cup" in early New Testament days were never separated from a meal. This is what was happening in Jerusalem when the believers were "breaking bread from house to house" and "taking their meals together with gladness and sincerity of heart" (Acts 2:46).

This is also why Paul inserted the word "supper" in his letter to the Corinthians between the breaking of bread and the participation in the cup. The apostle reminds us that Jesus *first* took the bread and "broke it" and said—"'This is my body, which is for you; do this in remembrance of me'" (1 Cor. 11:24). Paul then states—"In the same way he took the cup also, *after supper,* saying, 'This cup is the new covenant in My blood; do this, as often as you drink it, in remembrance of Me'" (1 Cor. 11:25).

At some point, Christians moved from a "full meal" in the home setting to a "token meal" in a public meeting place. The token meal has become the primary way in which we participate in what we call "The Lord's Supper." In actuality, it is not a "supper" in the true sense of that word. On the other hand, the meaning is still there—even though it may be a token meal involving a small piece of bread and a little cup of juice.

The Family—The Church in Miniature. The family setting provides us with a unique opportunity to participate in the Lord's Supper to a great extent in the way it was practiced in the first century. As fathers, we have opportunity to lead our families in this experience. Personally, I like to take the bread which is a part of the evening meal and have a preliminary "breaking of the bread" before the main meal. We thank the Lord for the broken bread—which symbolizes Christ's broken body. Following that experience, we thank the Lord for the food. Then, we have the "supper"—the main meal.

Following the supper, I personally like to take a pitcher of juice, pour it into various glasses and pass the juice around the table as we participate in drinking together—remembering the shed blood of Jesus Christ. Again, we thank the Lord for His shed blood. The whole experience can be culminated with a hymn, just as Jesus did many years ago with His disciples.

By utilizing this family setting, it's possible to recreate the unique fellowship with one another and the fellowship New Testament believers had with God.

"But, shouldn't we meet in a church building?" There are some Christians who believe that it is inappropriate to have a communion service outside of a church building. These people, however, fail to realize that church buildings did not come into existence until somewhere in the second and third centuries. The church initially met in homes. In fact, individual family units formed the basis of New Testament churches.

"But, you're not a deacon!" Some people believe that only official church leaders can conduct communion services. Again, the Scriptures contradict this conclusion. In fact, since many individual homes formed the basis of the New Testament church, fathers were the spiritual leaders in that setting. In that sense, each individual family unit was a church in miniature.

Circumcision of the Heart

Even in Old Testament days, circumcision was a means to help people experience an internal reality. This is why Paul wrote that "they are not all Israel who are descended from Israel" (Rom. 9:6). Earlier in his letter to the Romans, Paul made this point even clearer:

For he is not a Jew who is one outwardly; neither is circumcision that which is outward in the flesh. But he is a Jew who is one inwardly; and *circumcision is that which is of the heart,* by the Spirit, not by the letter; and his praise is not from men, but from God. (Rom. 2:28–29)

"Made without Hands." Circumcision is no longer necessary as an ordinance from God. Though it is certainly medically recommended, it has no spiritual significance since Christ came to fulfill the demands of God's law. In Christ we "have been made complete." In Christ we have been "circumcised with a *circumcision made without hands"* (Col. 2:10–11). And today we are to reveal His grace through our total being—body, soul, and spirit (Rom. 12:1–2). We are His children, and people everywhere should know that we are different, not because of the "circumcision of our flesh" but because of the "circumcision of our hearts."

"A New and Living Way." Indeed, we, like Moses and Joshua, are standing on holy ground—daily! Through Christ we can enter into the very presence of God. With confidence we can "enter the holy place by the blood of Jesus, by a new and living way which He inaugurated for us through the veil, that is, His flesh" (Heb. 10:19–20).

We need not fear. We need not remove our shoes or maintain a particular posture. But always we should "draw near with a sincere heart in full assurance of faith" (Heb. 10:22) and always we should reflect His character and His love so that all men will know that we are children of God.

Precious Memories

Though my early church background left much to be desired when measured by biblical standards, there are some things I will never forget. The church ordinances—baptism and communion—those things we do "in remembrance" of what God has done for us, were special to me. I'll never forget my own baptismal service. The death and resurrection of Christ became very real. Though I was quite confused in other doctrinal areas in my Christian life, I understood the true meaning of the ordinances.

Today these ordinances are even more meaningful to me. One thing that has made them more meaningful is when I realized in a new way that they are not only for Christians to practice but for non-Christians to see. Properly performed in the presence of unbelievers, these ordinances can become a dynamic means for communicating the gospel of Jesus Christ.

Points of Action

➤ Have you been baptized since you became a Christian? Furthermore, if you have children, have you taken responsibility to make sure that your children come to Christ and are baptized?

➤ Are you a part of a group where you regularly remember the Lord through holy communion?

➤ Are you truly converted to Jesus Christ, having been circumcised in heart through the operation of the Holy Spirit? Furthermore, as a Christian, are you reflecting Christ's righteousness and love to all people, revealing that you are indeed a new person in Christ?

A Man's Man Is a Godly Man

Reread the questions under Points of Action. As you do, ask the Holy Spirit to impress on your heart one lesson you need to apply more effectively in your life. Then write out a specific goal. For example, you may never have been baptized since you put your faith in Jesus Christ and became a Christian. Or perhaps, you have children who are believers but they have never been baptized.

Set a Goal

With God's help, I will begin immediately to carry out the following goal in my life:

_____

_____

_____

_____

Memorize the Following Scripture

For in Him all the fullness of Deity dwells in bodily form, and in Him you have been made complete, and He is the head over all rule and authority; and in Him you were also circumcised with a circumcision made without hands, in the removal of the body of the flesh by the circumcision of Christ; having been buried with Him in baptism, in which you were also raised up with Him through faith in the working of God, who raised Him from the dead.
COLOSSIANS 2:9–12

Chapter 7

The Walls Came Tumblin' Down
Read Joshua 6:1–27

One thing that used to be difficult for me to understand and accept was God's judgment on pagan people in the Old Testament. Perhaps you have questions too.

Is God Unjust?

Some people conclude (I did at one time) that the Lord suddenly descended on the Caananite people without warning and wiped them off the face of the earth. Not so! Remember Rahab's report to the spies? Her people had known about the God of Israel for at least forty years. They had heard of all He had done to the Egyptians because of their sins. They knew what had happened to those who opposed Israel in the wilderness (Josh. 2:10–11).

And now they also knew about the miracle at the Jordan River. "Their hearts melted" with fear. "There was no spirit in them any longer"—they were literally demoralized (5:1).

Another Opportunity to Repent

What we are going to see in this chapter is that God gave the people of Jericho seven more days to turn from their sins. You see, God never judged people (including Sodom and Gomorrah) without warning them numerous times that He was going to destroy them because of their idolatry and immorality. Again and again we see God's love, grace, mercy, and patience in the Old Testament. It's true that few people repented, but when they did, God relented and preserved them.

It's not God's desire to judge people. His attitude has been the same as that expressed by the apostle Peter. He does not want "any to perish but for all to come to repentance" (2 Pet. 3:9).

Moving Forward!

The children of Israel were now in the land of Canaan—a dream come true! God again demonstrated His great power (through the miracle at Jordan). The Lord reminded them of His unconditional covenant with them (through the rite of circumcision). He also reminded them of His grace in delivering them from Egyptian bondage (through the Passover). They were now ready to take the land through military advancement. The city of Jericho was, by God's direct command, to be their first target.

Taking No Chances

The people in Jericho were terribly frightened, according to the message Rahab conveyed to Israel (Josh. 2:10–11). Not only had they heard about the Red Sea fiasco for the pursuing Egyptians some forty years earlier, but more recently they had received reports of how the two kings of the Amorites beyond Jordan, along with all their people, had been literally wiped off the face of the earth (Num. 21:33–35). When God rolled back the waters of the rushing and swirling Jordan River so Israel could cross on dry ground, they were completely demoralized (Josh. 5:1). Thus we read "Jericho was tightly shut because of the sons of Israel" and "no one went out and no one came in" (6:1).

"The Arm of Flesh Will Fail You"

Somehow the people in Jericho believed they could protect themselves from the God of Israel by man-made walls—not facing the fact that those walls of stone were just as much subject to God's power as the waters of the Red Sea and the Jordan River. If God can control and manipulate natural phenomena, how much more can He destroy man-made structures and thwart bows and arrows?

Foolish? Yes! But how common for men and women who do not know God and who are blinded by their self-centered lifestyles and pagan religions. As the songwriter so appropriately stated, "The arm of flesh will fail you."

God Said "March!"

Attacking Jericho was not a human idea that originated in Joshua's mind. It was God's will and command to Israel. The Lord's instructions were very specific, down to the last detail.

Getting Ready

God had prepared Joshua in a special way for this battle. As we've already seen, the process began in the previous chapter. "The captain of the Lord's host"—who was probably God Himself in human form—appeared to Joshua while he was surveying Jericho. Revealing Himself as a man prepared for battle, the Lord instructed Joshua to remove his sandals from his feet because the place where he was standing was holy ground (5:13–15).[1]

The initial preparation for this battle was spiritual. It was no ordinary strategy. What God was about to command Joshua to do was strange indeed compared to the battle techniques he had used on previous occasions. In fact, all of Israel needed to be prepared spiritually and psychologically for what would appear to be a ridiculous and bizarre battle plan.

Moving Ahead by Faith

Joshua was ready! His response was immediate! How could he doubt now? Had God not proved faithful in the face of impossible situations? If the Lord could roll back the waters of Jordan, it would be no problem for Him to get the Israelites inside the walls of Jericho, even though the strategy—from a human perspective—made no sense at all.

Verses 2–5 in chapter 6 are a continuation of God's revelation in verses 13–15 in chapter 5 when Joshua encountered the "captain of the Lord's host." Once the Lord had prepared Joshua spiritually, He gave him specific instructions for attacking Jericho:

> "See, I have given Jericho into your hand, with its king and the valiant warriors. And you shall march around the city, all the men of war circling the city once. You shall do so for six days. Also seven priests shall carry seven trumpets of rams' horns before the ark; then on the seventh day you shall march around the city seven times, and the priests shall blow the trumpets. And it shall be that when they make a long blast with the ram's horn, and when you hear the sound of the trumpet, all the people shall shout with a great shout; and the wall of the city will fall down flat, and the people will go up every man straight ahead." (6:2–5)

The Plan Unfolds

What follows in this chapter are God's instructions fleshed out in the lives of the children of Israel (vv. 6–19). Joshua and the people obeyed God's orders to the last detail. Consequently, they captured the city just as the Lord said they would.

They Marched in Total Silence!

Imagine what must have been going through the minds of the inhabitants of Jericho as they watched the children of Israel from inside their fortressed walls. Soldiers were marching around the city. In the middle of the procession, priests of God carried the Ark of the Covenant, and still others blew rams' horns. But, just as God had commanded, none of the Israelites said a word. They marched in total silence.

What a Strange Sight!

The same thing happened the second day, and the third. It continued until six days elapsed. And then came the seventh day. But this was different. As before, they began the procession in the morning, but the soldiers of Israel didn't return to camp after encircling the walls once. It was indeed a strange sight! They marched around a second time and a third—until they had circled the city seven complete times. By now there must have been utter consternation inside the walls. What was happening? What was this unbelievable demonstration?

Then It Happened!

At Joshua's command and for the first time in a week, the Israelites' voices rang out. At the sound of the trumpet, they shouted a "great shout" and the walls of Jericho came crashing to the ground (v. 20).

Why did these huge walls—wide enough to provide a foundation for Rahab's home—come tumbling down with so little effort? Some scholars believe that they collapsed because of an earthquake, since such natural phenomena are prevalent in this geographical region. Perhaps this is true, for it would be no problem for God to synchronize supernaturally an earthquake with the shout that went up from Israel's army. Whatever it was, however—whether natural earthquake, supernatural earthquake, or no earthquake at all—God had worked another miracle for Israel.[2]

The Battle Was the Lord's!

When the walls collapsed, the army of Israel entered Jericho and began to destroy their enemies (vv. 20–27). Caught off guard by this strange strategy, the people in the city were confused and had no time to prepare to avoid the catastrophe.

God was on Israel's side all the way—both outside and inside the city. It was a supernatural victory. God had said, "'I have given Jericho into your hand'" (6:2). The death blow that fell on the inhabitants of Jericho was a judgment from God because of their sin and their unrepentant hearts. Although these people fell at the hands of the men of Israel, the victory was God's. Israel was merely the vessel He used to accomplish His purpose.

Rahab and Her Family Were Saved!

Rahab and those members of her family who responded to her warning of coming judgment were spared. Just as the spies instructed, she had gathered her relatives into her house and hung the scarlet rope in the window. Consequently, Joshua honored her obedience. In fact, he ordered the two spies whose lives she had saved to enter Jericho and bring Rahab and her whole family outside of the city and into the camp of Israel. Thus, we read—

> Rahab the harlot and her father's household and all she had, Joshua spared; and she has lived in the midst of Israel to this day, for she hid the messengers whom Joshua sent to spy out Jericho. (6:25)

Reflections on God's Strategy

There are various interpretations in attempting to explain God's war strategy against the people of Jericho. Why would He have Israel march around Jericho for seven days? Some believe the process was solely for Israel—to teach them faith and obedience. Certainly this was involved. It did take faith for these men to obey God's instructions instead of following their natural tendency to engage in ordinary tactics of warfare.

I believe there's another reason—one that relates to God's compassion for the unsaved. We must remember that God did not choose Israel to show favoritism or partiality, or to demonstrate a national and narrow concern for mankind. Rather, He chose Israel to be His means to convey to *all nations* His existence, His sovereignty, His righteousness and His holiness. He chose Israel to bear the message that He was willing to save all those—Jew or Gentile—who would truly call upon Him. Israel was to become God's unique and dramatic visual to convey that He is a loving and merciful God, ready to save all people from their sins, even though—as Paul reminded the Romans—they did not see fit to acknowledge Him (Rom. 1:28).

Solomon's Prayer

Many years later, when Solomon prayed to dedicate the Temple, he summarized God's love for all people very clearly:

> "Also concerning the foreigner who is not of Thy people Israel, when he comes from a far country for Thy name's sake (for they will hear of Thy great name and Thy mighty hand, and of Thine outstretched arm); when he comes and prays toward this house, hear Thou in heaven Thy dwelling place, and do according to all for which the foreigner calls to Thee, *in order that all the peoples of the earth may know Thy name, to fear Thee, as do Thy people Israel.*" (1 Kings 8:41–43)

One More Chance

God was giving the Canaanites of Jericho one more chance to turn from their sins and their wicked ways. As Israel marched around the walls of Jericho, it seems that God was saying once for all, "Judgment is coming! Repent and turn from your sins!" With each day, the final hour was growing closer, and it reached a grand crescendo on the seventh day as the people marched around the city seven times. And seven times, God was saying, "Repent!"

Would God Have Changed His Mind?

There are numerous events in the Old Testament to indicate that if the people in Jericho had flung open the gates and begged for mercy, turning to God and asking for forgiveness, the Lord would have relented. When Jonah warned the people of Nineveh that in "yet forty days" God would pronounce judgment on them, the people repented and God relented (Jon. 3:4–10).

God also would have spared Sodom and Gomorrah. His reticence to bring judgment on these cities is clearly seen in His willingness to relent when Abraham asked Him to spare the cities if fifty righteous people could be found. Then Abraham moved the number down to forty-five, to forty, to thirty, to twenty and finally to ten. Even so, God promised He would not destroy Sodom and Gomorrah if Abraham could find just ten righteous people (Gen. 18:23–32). Of course, there were not even ten. And God's judgment fell on these wicked people—just as it did on the inhabitants of Jericho.

Jericho Was Another Warning

Remember too that God's judgment on Jericho was just one additional warning to the other Canaanite cities. Their turn was coming. Israel was on the march—at the command of God. And with each death blow God was saying, "Repent! Repent! Repent! Turn from your wicked ways, your immoralities, your false gods, your child sacrifices and your numerous other evil deeds. And if you do, I'll preserve you as I did Rahab the harlot and her whole family."

Becoming God's Man Today

Principles to Live By

Principle 1. Scoffers have always existed no matter how much light they have.

Even in New Testament days, just a few short years after Christ walked on this earth, teaching and working miracles, there were mockers who rejected the signs of coming judgment. Listen to the words of Peter:

> Where is the promise of His coming? For ever since the fathers fell asleep, all continues just as it was from the beginning of creation.
>
> For when they maintain this, it escapes their notice that by the word of God the heavens existed long ago and the earth was formed out of water and by water, through which the world at that time was destroyed, being flooded with water. But the present heavens and earth by His word are being reserved for fire, kept for the day of judgment and destruction of ungodly men.
>
> But do not let this one fact escape your notice, beloved, that with the Lord one day is as a thousand years, and a thousand years as one day. The Lord is not slow about His promise, as some count slowness, but is patient toward you, *not wishing for any to perish but for all to come to repentance.* But the day of the Lord will come like a thief in which the heavens will pass away with a roar and the elements will be destroyed with intense heat, and the earth and its works will be burned up. (2 Pet. 3:4–10)

Principle 2. God is still patient and long-suffering with people who reject Him.

"The Lord . . . is patient . . . not wishing for any to perish but for all to come to repentance" (2 Pet. 3:9). This is still God's attitude, just as it was His attitude toward the people of Canaan. It has been His attitude toward the whole world since the day Adam and Eve sinned in the Garden. Through Abraham and Israel, and in these last days through Jesus Christ, He has been reaching out to all people. His long-suffering is obvious.

Jesus Christ is still waiting for people to turn to Him. In His mysterious and sovereign way, He is delaying His return to earth because He desires that all people be saved. Obviously, not all will turn to Him. But some will—just like Rahab and her family. Jesus said that the road that leads to destruction is wide and many follow that road. He also stated that the road that leads to eternal life is narrow and few follow that path (Matt. 7:13–14). The people of Jericho illustrate those who choose the wide path. Rahab and her family certainly illustrate those who choose the narrow way.

What about you? Have you personally received Jesus Christ to be your Savior from sin? Don't put off this important decision any longer. Receive Him and His forgiveness today. Pray this prayer with sincerity and He will indeed give you eternal life:

> Father, I have sinned. Though my sins may not be as great as the Canaanites of old, I am still sinful and separated from you. Thank You for dying for my sins. I now receive You as my own personal Lord and Savior. Thank You for accepting me, for saving me and for giving me eternal life.

Principle 3. God uses people to reach people.

In the whole of Scripture, we see five dimensions to God's missionary strategy:

Being

What we "are" as a local body of believers is foundational to having an effective evangelistic outreach into our local community. "Being" what Christ commanded and prayed for in John's Gospel should serve as a dynamic bridge to the world. Our love for one another (John 13:34–35), bearing the fruit of righteousness (15:8) and unity (17:20–23) all attract non-Christians, first to us, and then to Jesus Christ, the One who has made us what we are. In essence, this was also God's plan for the nation of Israel in the Old Testament. They were to love God with all their hearts and their neighbors as themselves (Mark 12:28–31).

How much are you doing to contribute to the love and unity in your church?

Going

Though "being" is foundational and essential for effective community outreach, it is only the beginning point. "Body visibility" only lays the groundwork for personal verbalization. Non-Christians can only understand and comprehend the gospel as they hear it explained.

How much are you involved in "going" to those who need to hear the message (Matt. 28:19–20)?

Sending

Not all Christians are called upon to leave their homes and communities in order to be missionaries or evangelists. In fact, most of the New Testament Christians who were converted to Christ from various pagan communities never left those communities. Rather, God's plan was that they remain where they were and become a dynamic corporate witness to the rest of their immediate community. However, His plan also was that there would be those who would go out from among them to carry the message of the gospel personally into the community and to the ends of the earth, supported both in prayer and finances by those who remain behind.

How much are you involved in "sending" others to preach the gospel to those who have not heard?

Giving

Financially supporting those who desire to serve Jesus Christ full-time as pastors and missionaries is just as much a part of carrying out the Great Commission as "going." From a Christian point of view, we cannot conscientiously send people out without meeting their physical needs and providing them with financial security. All of us are to give systematically, proportionally and cheerfully (2 Cor. 9:6–7).

How much are you utilizing your financial resources to achieve God's purposes in this world?

Praying

Christians are to pray about many things—about *all* things (Phil. 4:6). But there are many New Testament examples that tell us we are to pray for those who represent us as evangelists and missionaries. Paul requested that kind of prayer when he wrote to the Ephesians (6:19–20).

How faithful are you in praying for missionaries and others who share the gospel?

Points of Action

➤ To what extent am I contributing to the dynamic body life and witness of my church?

➤ To what extent am I personally sharing Christ with non-Christians?

➤ To what extent am I encouraging others to serve in the area of missionary outreach?

➤ To what extent am I financially supporting missions?

➤ To what extent am I praying for those who go?

A Man's Man Is a Godly Man

Reread the questions under Points of Action. As you do, ask the Holy Spirit to impress on your heart one lesson you need to apply more effectively in your life. Then write out a specific goal. For example, you may not be a regular and proportionate giver to your church in order to support missions outreach. This has never been a part of your Christian discipline. Or, perhaps you once did but have failed to be consistently obedient in this area of your life. You also know that this is a poor model to your wife and to your children.

Set a Goal

With God's help, I will begin immediately to carry out the following goal in my life:

_____

_____

_____

Memorize the Following Scripture

"But you shall receive power when the Holy Spirit has come upon you; and you shall be My witnesses both in Jerusalem, and in all Judea and Samaria, and even to the remotest part of the earth."

ACTS 1:8

Chapter 8

A Terrible Tragedy
Read Joshua 7:1–26

*A*s a young person growing up in my particular religious background, my view of God was somewhat distorted. Unfortunately, I saw Him more as a God of wrath than a God of love. Actually, we see His long-suffering and patience with the weaknesses of mankind far more often in the Bible than His judgments.

There are occasions, however, when God administered severe punishment for sin. This is particularly true when His people engaged in flagrant disobedience in the full light of His divine revelation. For God to allow the sin to go unnoticed and unpunished in these instances would have caused the masses to lose respect for Him and His Word.

The Miracle at Jericho

What a great victory for Joshua and the armies of Israel! From a human point of view, there was no way to explain the event. It was indeed another fantastic miracle—equal in intensity, drama and divine significance to the Red Sea experience and Israel's entrance into Canaan through the Jordan River.

Jericho was the first city to fall under the judgment of God. The next would be Ai, another Canaanite city that lay about ten miles west of Jericho. Whatever fear and ambivalence the children of Israel may have felt when they first approached Jericho faded away in the light of their astounding victory.

A Sobering Story

In spite of the great victory at Jericho, lurking in the shadows was a serious problem—a problem of sin that would soon turn the Israelites' spirit of confidence into internal anxiety, emotional confusion and doubt. A man by the name of Achan violated some of God's specific instructions regarding the spoils of Jericho. Consequently, Israel was about to experience a humiliating defeat.

Achan's Flagrant Disobedience

When the Lord initially gave Joshua instructions regarding the way Israel was to attack and capture Jericho, He had stated very specifically that the entire city was "under the ban." Everything and everyone in the city—except for Rahab and her family—must be destroyed and burned with fire. There was only one exception: "All the silver and gold and articles of bronze and iron" were to be considered "holy to the LORD" and were to "go into the treasury of the LORD" (6:19).

Achan, an Israelite from the tribe of Judah, deliberately disregarded God's command. Secretly, he "took some of the things under the ban" and hid them in his tent. Consequently, God's anger "burned against the sons of Israel" (7:1).

For God to place people and things "under the ban" was not a new phenomenon in Israel. In fact, it was written into the laws given to Israel at Sinai (Lev. 27:29). And when Moses reviewed the law prior to their entrance into Canaan, he explained to Israel and warned them regarding the ban:

> "And the LORD your God will clear away these nations before you little by little. . . . The graven images of their gods you are to burn with fire; you shall not covet the silver or the gold

that is on them, *nor take it for yourselves,* lest you be snared by it, for it is an abomination to the Lord your God. And you shall not bring an abomination into your house, and like it come under the *ban*; you shall utterly detest it and you shall utterly abhor it, for it is something *banned.*" (Deut. 7:22, 25–26)

God placed Jericho and everything in it under this ban. In full awareness of God's warning through Moses and now through Joshua regarding what would happen to him and his whole household, Achan took some of the silver and the gold and fine clothes from Jericho and concealed them in his tent. Achan flagrantly, and in the full light of God's revelation, violated His holy law! In God's sight, it was an act of idolatry and wickedness that must be punished.

Israel's Humiliating Defeat

Following Israel's tremendous victory in Jericho, Joshua took immediate steps to conquer the city of Ai. He sent some men to spy out the city. When they returned, their report to Joshua radiated confidence and self-assurance: "'Do not let all the people go up,'" they said. "'Only about two or three thousand men need go up to Ai; do not make all the people toil up there, for they are few'" (7:3).

Unfortunately, Joshua took these men at their word! He sent a small band of men to capture this city. And to his amazement, the men of Ai struck back and defeated Israel.

Joshua and all the children of Israel were nonplussed. They couldn't believe their eyes. They were so frightened that their hearts "melted and became as water" (v. 5).

What happened? No one really knew—except God and Achan! The root problem was the man's sin.

But there were some other problems too. Though Achan was primarily at fault, there were leaders in Israel who were guilty of taking matters into their own hands.

Israel had come off of an unbelievable victory—resulting in feelings of pride and arrogance. In fact, the men who were sent to spy on Ai were so sure of themselves they didn't take time to get all the facts. They woefully misjudged the number of armed warriors in Ai! Even more tragic, they failed to remember that it was God who had given them the victory in Jericho—not their great wisdom and human strategies.

Have you ever faced this kind of problem in your own life? I have! I am most vulnerable following some great accomplishment or victory. How easy it is at those times to misjudge, to become overly self-assured, to rely upon my own strengths and abilities! And frequently God has to teach me—through allowing defeat in my life—that I must maintain an intricate balance between having confidence in myself and continually trusting in God to guide me and help me to discern His perfect will. Unfortunately, I sometimes learn that lesson through failure.

How quickly we can stumble and fall! Often it happens when we feel the most successful in our Christian experience. In the midst of our failure, it's sometimes difficult to understand the problem or to know how to approach the situation with spiritual perspective. This was Joshua's problem, too!

Joshua's Painful Dismay

Joshua was caught totally off guard when Israel was defeated by the men from Ai. His emotions quickly took over and "he tore his clothes and fell to the earth." Though outwardly humble, in reality, he was more concerned about his own feelings of dismay than he was to get to the root of the problem. This is apparent from his prayer:

> And Joshua said, "Alas, O LORD God, why didst Thou ever bring this people over the Jordan, only to deliver us into the hand of the Amorites, to destroy us? If only we had been willing to dwell beyond the Jordan! Oh Lord, what can I say since Israel has turned their back before their enemies? For

the Canaanites and all the inhabitants of the land will hear of it, and they will surround us and cut off our name from the earth. And what wilt Thou do for Thy great name?" (7:7–9)

Clearly, Joshua had lost perspective. In the midst of defeat he forgot God's promise that He was going to give them the land. Had not the Lord just instructed Joshua to circumcise the sons of Israel as a sign of that promise? Had they not just remembered their great deliverance from Egypt with the Passover? And what about the memorial stones? And most of all, what about Jericho? Would God so quickly forsake them?

Joshua's reactions reveal that he was human—just like you and me. There is a fine line between the feelings of success and failure. One moment we can be elated with our achievements. And a short time later we can be depressed over our failures. When depressed and dismayed, we often lose sight of God's overall plan for our lives—His promises, His previous victories and His divine presence with us. Often God has to deal with us just as He did with Joshua. He has to remind us of the facts!

The Lord's Specific Directions

Though Joshua's emotions were very real and painful, they were surface feelings! He was too mature a man to go down in deep despair and defeat! God knew he was feeling sorry for himself. Consequently the Lord dealt with him at that level! "'Rise up!'" the Lord said. "'Why is it that you have fallen on your face?'" (v. 10).

With this command and question, the Lord indicated that Joshua should have known what was wrong. Had he stopped to think for a moment, he would have concluded that someone had violated God's law regarding the ban on Jericho. Thus the Lord answered His own question directly and to the point:

"Israel has sinned, and they have also transgressed My covenant which I commanded them. And they have even taken some of the things under the ban and have both stolen and deceived. Moreover, they have also put them among their own things. Therefore the sons of Israel cannot stand before their enemies; they turn their backs before their enemies, for they have become accursed. I will not be with you anymore unless you destroy the things under the ban from your midst." (vv. 11–12)

The Lord followed this general revelation with some very specific instructions for solving the problem. Rather than immediately identifying Achan and those involved with him, the Lord spelled out a step-by-step method for discovering the culprit. First, all the children of Israel were to consecrate themselves before the Lord (v. 13). All of them were to search their hearts, for in reality they were all guilty of pride and having failed to trust God following their victory at Jericho.

The Lord next revealed the procedure for discovering Achan:

"In the morning then you shall come near by your *tribes*. And it shall be that the tribe which the LORD takes by lot shall come near by *families*, and the family which the LORD takes shall come near by *households*, and the household which the LORD takes shall come near *man by man*." (v. 14)

Achan's Tragic Discovery

Think for a moment why God used this unfolding tactic. Why didn't He just identify Achan and the others involved? Personally I believe there are two reasons. *First,* God wanted Israel to observe the process and never to forget. As each lot fell and as each tribe, family, and household was identified, all Israel would have a chance to think hard and long about the seriousness of violating God's commandments. Short memories often need dramatic experiences!

Second, I believe God, in His divine love and mercy, was once again offering a way of escape to a man who had woefully disobeyed Him. Had Achan immediately confessed and truly repented of his sin, he and his whole household might have been spared! It would be consistent with God's nature to do this, for years later He pardoned David, the king of Israel, who committed two horrible sins which should have brought death. But because of David's repentant heart, the Lord spared him.

God was giving Achan time—just as He had done for the people of Jericho. His tribe was identified, his family, and finally his household! Still Achan did not confess! It was only after the lot fell on him that he acknowledged his sin. He waited until his back was against the wall. He had no choice. His confession was forced! It was too late—just as it will be for many some day when every knee shall bow before God and acknowledge who He is (Phil. 2:10–11).

God's Awful Judgment—Death

The end of this story is tragic! Achan and his family and everything he owned, including what he had stolen, were completely destroyed and burned with fire (Josh. 7:22–26). Because Achan identified himself with the ban God placed on Jericho, he and his whole household were brought under the same judgment.

Becoming God's Man Today

Principles to Live By

Principle 1. God is a holy God!

This Old Testament passage is one of the most sobering in all the Bible. It teaches us that God indeed is a holy God. Though He is patient and long-suffering, He cannot persistently tolerate sin, especially when it is flagrantly committed in the light of His full and direct revelation.

Principle 2. The more light we have, the more we are accountable.

This is dramatically illustrated in the life of Achan. God revealed Himself again and again, not only through visible signs and miracles but by direct commands. Years before, He warned Israel against this kind of sin, that to indulge in it would bring judgment on an entire household. To make sure they understood the seriousness of this law, God reviewed this matter for Israel before they entered Jericho (6:18). And it was in the full light of God's direct warning that Achan disobeyed God! In many respects, it would be as serious as walking into the holy of holies in the Tabernacle and pushing the ark of the Covenant to the ground, replacing it with a pagan idol. It was a very serious form of idolatry.

Principle 3. Beware of flagrant lying.

Notice what happened to Ananias and Sapphira in the New Testament. In the midst of the dramatic events in the church at Jerusalem, Satan caused them "to lie to the Holy Spirit." Consequently, they were severely judged by God. Both of them died on the spot! And when it happened, "great fear came upon the whole church, and upon all who heard" about it (Acts 5:11).

Principle 4. Can this kind of judgment happen today?

To answer this question, we need to review what Paul wrote in his Corinthian letter. Disturbed with the leaders who were destroying the unity in the church, he issued a stern warning:

> Do you not know [all of you] that you are a temple [church] of God and that the Spirit of God dwells in you [all of you]? If any man destroys the temple [the church] of God, God will destroy him, for the temple [the church] of God is holy, and that is what you are [all of you]. (1 Cor. 3:16–17)

I know of times when God has severely judged Christians who have flagrantly and deliberately destroyed unity in the church because of their own selfish and carnal motives. Though this may not involve death, it has been serious and painful judgment. In these cases, the sin has been so obvious that no one can misinterpret what has happened.

In conclusion, we must remind ourselves that even the Bible records very few times when God breaks through with this kind of judgment. But when He does, it falls on people who have willfully disobeyed God in the full light of His revealed will and power.

Principle 5. All have sinned!

Both of these stories teach all of us an important lesson. Yes, God is holy and He hates sin, but the primary lesson is that in a very real sense we are all under the ban—for we "all have sinned and fall short of the glory of God" (Rom. 3:23). Again Paul states, "There is none righteous, not even one" (v. 10).

This is why God instituted the sacrifice in the Old Testament. This is why He eventually sent His Son, Jesus Christ, to die once for all for the sins of the world. When we receive Jesus Christ—when we believe that He died for us personally—He justifies us and makes us righteous in His sight. The blood of Jesus Christ keeps on cleansing us from all sin (1 John 1:9).

Knowing that we are eternally forgiven does not, however, give us an excuse to continue to live in sin. If we deliberately disobey God, we'll suffer the consequences. We'll reap what we sow. As a loving heavenly Father, God will discipline us in order to bring us back into the center of His will. On the other hand, if we're not disciplined when we persistently sin, the Bible teaches that we may not be His children but illegitimate sons and daughters (Heb. 12:7–8).

Points of Action

Do You Know Christ Personally?

Can you say, "If I, _____ , died tonight, I know I would go to heaven and be with Christ forever"?

If you can say this, write your name in the blank. If you cannot and you want to know Christ, sincerely pray the following prayer:

"Father, I know that I am a sinner. I know I have failed You. I receive Your Son, Jesus Christ, to be my Lord and Savior from sin. Thank You for the gift of salvation."

If you prayed this prayer sincerely, write your name in the blank on the previous page.

Are You Living in God's Will?

There is a question all of us as Christians must ask ourselves—"Am I a believer who is willingly and deliberately living in sin?" If I am, God is displeased. He wants us to live holy and righteous lives.

Remember that if you are knowingly living in sin—if you are willingly violating God's laws—you will be disciplined. If you are, thank God, for you are His child! Acknowledge your sins and claim His forgiveness in Jesus Christ (1 John 1:9).

On the other hand, if you are living in sin and are not being disciplined in your conscience and in other areas of your life, then reevaluate your relationship to Jesus Christ. Is it real? Perhaps you're not truly saved.

Are You Taking Advantage of God's Grace?

Because God does not deal with your sin immediately does not mean that He never will. Don't forget that God is patient and long-suffering.

Take a few moments to reflect on your life. If you have just received Jesus Christ as your personal Savior, thank Him for His marvelous gift to you. Ask Him to help you grow in your Christian life.

If you are a Christian, and you know there are things in your life that are not proper for a Christian, take this moment to confess your sins to Him. Receive the forgiveness He has promised.

If you're walking with God and enjoying His presence, take a moment to worship and praise Him for all He has done for you.

A Man's Man Is a Godly Man

As you evaluate the following principles, pray and ask the Holy Spirit to impress on your heart one lesson you need to apply more effectively in your life. Then write out a specific goal. For example, you may have difficulty being completely honest. It's easy for you to twist the truth. You know this is wrong and sinful and that God will eventually discipline you for this sin.

➤ God is a holy God!

➤ The more light we have, the more we are accountable.

➤ Beware of being dishonest.

➤ God will eventually discipline us if we continue in sin.

Set a Goal

With God's help, I will begin immediately to carry out the following goal in my life:

_____

_____

_____

_____

Memorize the Following Scripture

If we confess our sins, He is faithful and righteous to forgive us our sins and to cleanse us from all unrighteousness.

1 JOHN 1:9

Chapter 9

Experiencing Victory God's Way
Read Joshua 8:1–29

*T*here's a divine mystery I'll never understand, at least while I'm living on this earth. But I know it is true. God can take the results of human weakness and, if we let Him, make them work together for good (Rom. 8:28).

How frequently I've seen this happen in my own life. Some of the greatest lessons I've learned resulted from my own mistakes or the mistakes others made that have touched my life.

We see this truth illustrated in this chapter. God took the results of Israel's sin and used it to give them victory at Ai.

Tragedy in Israel

The humiliating defeat of Israel by the inhabitants of Ai and the tragic events surrounding the household of Achan left Joshua fearful and brokenhearted. Not only must it have been horribly difficult to issue the order to execute Achan and his family, but Joshua was surrounded by thousands of discouraged and frustrated Israelites. Gloom and despair permeated all of Israel.

How Quickly It All Happened

Ever since the Lord spoke to Joshua following Moses' death, reassuring him of His blessings on him as the new leader of

Israel, Joshua had responded with courage and inner strength. He took God at His word. His fears dissipated and his faith was strong. He triumphantly guided the children of Israel across Jordan. He boldly led the army of Israel against Jericho, knowing they would be victorious.

But suddenly, within hours, Joshua found himself experiencing old frustrations and anxieties. His triumphant faith turned to immobilizing fear. He felt defeated and in despair. He saw no way out.

"I Will Not . . . Forsake You"

Even though a black cloud of depression gripped Joshua's soul and hovered over all Israel, God had not forsaken His servant or His people (1:5). He would not and could not! He had promised them the land if they would obey Him. And because Joshua carried out His commands regarding Achan, "the Lord turned from the fierceness of His anger" (7:26). Immediately God took steps to reassure Joshua that He indeed was with him and would help him lead Israel on to further victories.

Reverting to Old Ways

Though Joshua was not responsible for the sin that led to Israel's defeat, he was not without fault in the way he handled the maneuver against Ai. He took matters into his own hands rather than consulting the Lord for specific directions (v. 2). Furthermore, his response to their defeat did not reflect the mature man of God that he was. In a moment of weakness, he reverted to his old ways.

Reassurance!

Once God dealt with the original cause of the problem (see vv. 10–11), He quickly reassured Joshua that He had not forsaken him or the nation of Israel:

"Do not fear or be dismayed. Take all the people of war with you and arise, go up to Ai; see, I have given into your hand the king of Ai, *his people, his city, and his land.* And you shall do to Ai and its king just as you did to Jericho and its king." (8:1–2a)

With this direct and rather detailed revelation, God was helping Joshua overcome his deep sense of insecurity. He assured him a victory!

Reiteration

Note also that God's words of encouragement to Joshua to "not fear or be dismayed" were the very same words Moses spoke years before to the people in Kadesh-barnea before he sent the twelve men to spy out the land of Canaan (Deut. 1:21). They were also the same words Moses spoke to Joshua forty years later when he turned the reins of leadership over to this young man following Israel's wilderness experience (31:8). At this moment in Joshua's life, following this humiliating defeat, God specifically reminded Joshua of His promise.

Achan's sin, serious as it was, did not mean the Lord had forsaken Israel. Nor did Joshua's immature response mean that God would not continue to use him as the chosen leader.

This is indeed reassuring to all of us! God does not withdraw His blessings permanently when we fail Him. Rather, He lovingly disciplines us and helps us to refocus on His will for our lives. It's also reassuring that we are not totally responsible for others' failures when we are in charge. Personally, I can identify with Joshua. As a leader, I often blame myself for others' failures. Though I am accountable for my mistakes ("the buck stops here"), I need reassurances that I am not totally to blame.

A Different Strategy—but the Same Results

To make His point even more reassuring, the Lord told Joshua that Israel would be able to capture Ai just as they had captured Jericho. Their strategy would be different, but the results would be the same. Israel would emerge victorious.

There was one other difference. When they captured Jericho, everything was placed under the ban. But at Ai, the Lord promised that they would be able to keep of the spoils of the city (Josh. 8:2).

A Lesson for All of Us

How ironic! Had Achan waited, had he not allowed greed and selfishness to take over in his life, he would have been able to take all he wanted and needed when they captured Ai. Sadly, he moved out ahead of the Lord, took matters into his own hands, violated God's law and brought judgment on himself and his whole family.

A Strategic Plan

After reassuring Joshua that he had not forsaken Israel, the Lord told him how to capture Ai. They were to "set an ambush for the city behind it" (8:2b).[1]

Reading through verses 2–17 surfaces some unique problems regarding the specific details of the strategy. However, the following sequence seems to be the most consistent explanation, although there is a difference of opinion among competent Old Testament scholars.

A Commando Unit

Joshua selected thirty men, "valiant warriors, and sent them out at night" to camp behind the city of Ai (on the west side). These men comprised a commando unit that was to eventually enter the city and set it on fire (vv. 3–4).[2]

Backup Troops

Behind this contingent of men there was another ambuscade comprising five thousand men (v. 12). When Joshua gave the proper signal, they were to follow the thirty commandos into the city as the rear guard, adding support to the ambush (v. 13).[3]

Decoys

In order to set the stage for this surprise attack, Joshua used a deceptive tactic. He and a number of other men in Israel went up to Ai following the same route as before. They camped overnight in the valley north of Ai in full view of their enemies.

It Worked

When the king of Ai saw what was happening, he ordered his own army to attack Israel just as they had done previously. Since he knew nothing of the Israelites who were waiting to attack from the west, he held none of his men back (v. 14).

The plan worked perfectly. Joshua and his men "pretended to be beaten before them." They retreated and the men of Ai pursued them, leaving the city unguarded (vv. 15–17). At just the right moment, Joshua signaled the attack from the rear (v. 18).[4] He raised his javelin and evidently men stationed at various distances formed a visual line that signaled the message to the commando units.

Attack they did! They entered Ai without resistance and "quickly set the city on fire" (v. 19).

Caught by Surprise

Imagine the look on the faces of the men of Ai! Fear gripped their hearts! When they looked back, they saw billows of smoke rising into the sky. The whole city was in flames. And before they could gather their wits, Joshua and his men suddenly turned and attacked. The five thousand men who had followed the initial commando unit into the city from the west also moved right on through the city and attacked the men of Ai from behind. Consequently, they "were trapped in the midst of Israel" and were utterly destroyed (v. 22).

Judgment Falls

When Israel defeated the army of Ai, they brought God's judgment upon the entire population, as they had done in Jericho. We read that "all who fell that day, both men and women, were twelve thousand—all the people of Ai" (v. 25).

The king, however, was taken captive and delivered to Joshua. Later, he was executed and buried beneath a pile of stones at the entrance to the city (vv. 23, 29).

Ai had fallen! Once again God proved Himself faithful to Israel. Not only had they destroyed their enemies, but they received a reward. They were allowed to take "the cattle and the spoil of that city as plunder for themselves" (v. 27).

Becoming God's Man Today

Principles to Live By

There are at least three very clear and practical lessons that emerge from this story.

Principle 1. God will never forsake His children, no matter how much they have forsaken Him.

Though Israel had violated God's laws and though Joshua had initially responded to God's discipline immaturely, the Lord did not forsake them as they thought He would. True, He eventually judged Israel's persistent disobedience by scattering them "from one end of the earth to the other" (Deut. 28:64). But it's also true that God will ultimately keep His promise even to Israel in spite of their utter failure. He will gather them from "the ends of the earth" and eventually bring them into the land which their fathers possessed (30:45).

"Lo, I Am with You Always"

God's promise to be with His children is even more striking and binding in the New Testament. We read in Hebrews 13:5,

"For He Himself has said, 'I will never desert you, nor will I ever forsake you.'" And when the Lord gave His followers the Great Commission, He promised: "'And lo, I am with you *always*, even to the end of the age'" (Matt. 28:20).

"If God Is for Us, Who Is Against Us?"

The apostle Paul believed and taught this truth without qualification. Listen to his words in his letter to the Roman Christians:

> What then shall we say to these things? If God is for us, who is against us? . . . Who shall separate us from the love of Christ? Shall tribulation, or distress, or persecution, or famine, or nakedness, or peril, or sword? . . . But in all these things we overwhelmingly conquer through Him who loved us. For I am convinced that neither death, nor life, nor angels, nor principalities, nor things present, nor things to come, nor powers, nor height, nor depth, nor any other created thing, shall be able to separate us from the love of God, which is in Christ Jesus our Lord. (Rom. 8:31, 35, 37–39)

Disappointing God

Obviously, God is displeased and disappointed when we sin against Him, when we fail to do His will. But no sin or failure can ever separate us spiritually from God. He promised us eternal life and He cannot lie, no matter how much we fail Him.

Illegitimate Children

The Bible also teaches that no Christian who knows God's will and who has experienced God's saving grace can continue to live in flagrant sin without being disciplined. Hopefully, he will eventually acknowledge that sin and return to God's will (Heb. 12:11). As stated in the previous chapter, a true child of God *will* be disciplined by his heavenly Father. If we experience no discipline, the Bible states explicitly that we "are illegitimate children and not sons" (Heb. 12:8).

What about you? Are you flagrantly living outside the will of God? Perhaps you believe the Lord has forsaken you. Rest assured He has not. He is waiting for you to turn from your sins and to experience His forgiveness (1 John 1:9).

Perhaps your feelings of loneliness and your sense of being forsaken are in themselves a result of your sin. Your feelings of alienation can be part of the disciplinary process God has allowed in your life to cause you to turn once again to Him and walk in His will. God is patiently waiting for you to respond to His unconditional love and grace.

When you do, accept God's forgiveness and also forgive yourself. Then live in the joy of that forgiveness, constantly conforming your life to the life of Jesus Christ.

Principle 2. God can take the mistakes His children make and can turn them into positive results.

This is what the Lord did with Israel's mistake in trying to attack Ai when they were unprepared both spiritually and militarily. He eventually used the same strategy that originally brought defeat to Israel to deceive and trap the men of Ai.

Principle 3. God gives us freedom to develop a strategic plan but it must always be in harmony with His basic guidelines and principles.

When God gave Joshua a basic plan for attacking Ai, He evidently did not fill in all the "blank spaces." He gave Joshua freedom to devise additional plans that were in harmony with His general plan. However, Joshua was constantly alert to God's guidance as he developed and worked out that plan.

Today, God gives us clear guidelines and principles in His Word for carrying out His will in this world. When we work within these parameters, we have unusual freedom to develop unique strategies that He will bless. We must not, however, take matters into our own hands and neglect His revealed will for our lives.

Turning Lemons into Lemonade

Only God can take our mistakes and the results of those mistakes and make them "work together for good" (Rom. 8:28). This does not mean that we will not experience the negative effects of our failures, just as Israel did. Thirty-six choice men lost their lives because Israel walked outside of the will of God (7:5). Furthermore, fear and anxiety gripped their hearts. Morale was at a low ebb. They doubted God's love and forgot His promises.

But God changed all that for Israel. And He can do it for us, too! If we let Him, He can turn our blunders into blessings.

Points of Action

Read the following paraphrase of Romans 8:28–39. Personalize this message from the Lord by mentally or literally writing your name in each blank. Then thank God for these reassuring promises.

And we know that God causes all things to work together for good to _____ who loves God, to _____ who is called according to His purpose. For He foreknew _____ and He also predestined _____ to become conformed to the image of His Son, that He might be the first-born among many brethren. And when He predestined _____ He also called; and whom He called, He also justified; and _____ whom He justified He also glorified.

What then shall we say to these things? If God is for _____ who is against me? He who did not spare His own Son, but delivered Him up for _____,

how will He not also with Him freely give _____
all things? Who will bring a charge against _____?
God is the one who justifies; who is the one who con-
demns? Christ Jesus is He who died, yes, rather who was
raised, who is at the right hand of God, who also intercedes
for _____.

    Who shall separate _____ from the love
of Christ? Shall tribulation, or distress, or persecution, or
famine, or nakedness, or peril, or sword? . . . But in all these
things _____ can overwhelmingly con-
quer through Him who loved me. For I am convinced that
neither death, nor life, nor angels, nor principalities, nor
things present, nor things to come, nor powers, nor height,
nor depth, nor any other created thing, shall be able to
separate _____ from the love of God, which
is in Christ Jesus our Lord. (Rom. 8:28–39, paraphrase)

A Man's Man Is a Godly Man

As you evaluate the following principles, pray and ask the Holy
Spirit to impress on your heart one lesson you need to apply
more effectively in your life. Then write out a specific goal. For
example, you may have made some serious mistakes in your life.
Somehow you can't forgive yourself. You're having difficulty
seeing how God can take this negative experience and turn it
into a positive lesson in your life—even helping someone else
to avoid your mistake.

➤ God will never forsake His children, no matter how much
they have forsaken Him.

➤ God can take the mistakes His children make and can turn
them into positive results.

➤ God gives us freedom to develop a strategic plan, but it must
always be in harmony with His basic guidelines and principles.

Set a Goal

With God's help, I will begin immediately to carry out the following goal in my life:

_____

_____

_____

_____

_____

Memorize the Following Scripture

And we know that God causes all things to work together for good to those who love God, to those who are called according to His purpose.
                    ROMANS 8:28

Chapter 10

Back to Basics
Read Joshua 8:30–35

*I*f you've ever been involved in team sports, you know that a good coach always takes you back to basics. No matter how good a team is, it's important always to review the fundamentals.

I've personally played a lot of very competitive volleyball. When we were behind, the coaches called time-out and reviewed the basics:

"Make sure you get the serve in!" (You only score when your team serves.)

"Always work for a good set." (This sets up the spike.)

"Generally—not always—set the ball twice so you can spike the third hit." (This allows time to get good control of the ball and place.)

Invariably, practicing these basics makes the difference between winning and losing. And so it is in our spiritual life. In this chapter, we'll see Joshua taking the children of Israel back to basics in terms of God's laws.

Moving from Here to There

To get our attention, the Holy Spirit often directed scriptural authors to use sharp contrasts as a literary technique in recording various events. This is what we see in Joshua chapter 8, following

Israel's unusual victory at Ai. In fact, the contrast is so sharp, not only from a literary standpoint but also in geographical setting, that some critics of the Bible believe that events recorded in this passage are out of sequence and were added by another author. Unfortunately, these scholars miss the purpose the Lord had in mind when He directed the author of the Book of Joshua to transport Israel and the reader suddenly from Ai to Mount Ebal in Shechem. But this geographical contrast only forms a dramatic backdrop against which a spiritual contrast stands out clearly. What was that contrast?

Two Piles of Stone

The final event recorded regarding Israel's victory over Ai was the execution of the king of the city. His body was buried at the gate of Ai, under "a great heap of stones" (8:29) and immediately following this statement we read: "Then Joshua built an altar to the LORD, the God of Israel, in Mount Ebal" (v. 30).

The Contrast Is Striking!

At the gate of a defeated and desolate pagan city lay the body of a pagan king, memorialized with a pile of stones, symbolizing the futility of worshiping the false gods of the Canaanites. But at Mount Ebal—in the very center of the land of Canaan—we see Joshua constructing an altar (also a pile of stones) to the God of Israel, symbolizing the blessings and protection that come from worshiping the one true God, "the God of Israel."[1]

There's More Here

This is not just a contrast between paganism and Judaism. Joshua learned a very important lesson based on his personal relationship with God and in his relationship to Israel as their political, military and—most importantly—their spiritual leader. He had experienced a great and rewarding victory at

Jericho (Josh. 6), contrasted by a humiliating and traumatic defeat at Ai (chap. 7).

Though Joshua was not directly responsible for Israel's failure, his initial response to the crisis (7:6–9) served as a rather painful reminder that it is very easy to forget quickly God's promises and the conditions He attaches to those promises. This is particularly true during times of great successes and victories. And God's method for reminding Joshua of His initial conversation with this new leader of Israel was to allow him to experience some of the old fears and anxieties that had plagued him when Moses' mantle fell on his shoulders.

Don't Misunderstand

God was not responsible for Achan's sin nor Israel's failure. As only the Lord can do, He simply took what was human failure, weakness, and sin and used it for good, particularly in the life of Israel. In the midst of this crisis, Joshua experienced the old fears that had gripped him following Moses' death. With those fears came a reminder of what God had promised in the midst of his human weakness: "'Be strong and courageous, for you shall give this people possession of the land which I swore to their fathers to give them.'" (1:6; see also 8:1–2)

God's Conditions for Success

Not only did Joshua's emotional and spiritual crisis remind him of God's promises but also of God's conditions for success—five direct commands that relate specifically to what was about to happen at Mount Ebal.

Let's Review

In those early days of trauma following Moses' death, God said, "'You shall give this people possession of the land'" (1:6). But here were God's conditions:

First, "Be careful to do according to all the law." [then]

Second, "Do not turn from it to the right or to the left" (1:7).

Third, "This book of the law shall not depart from your mouth." [then]

Fourth, "You shall meditate on it day and night." [and finally]

Fifth, "Be careful to do according to all that is written in it" (1:8).

The Connection Is Clear

Before the children of Israel ever entered the Promised Land, Moses told them specifically to build an altar to the Lord at Mount Ebal (Deut. 27:4–7).

You see, Joshua was obeying God's command. And in the process, we see he was also reviewing God's Word to make sure Israel would continue "to do according to all the law . . . according to all that is written in it." Joshua, particularly, did not want to face another Ai and the kind of tragic events surrounding Achan's household and Israel's humiliating defeat.

It is clear from the flow of events recorded thus far that what happened at Mount Ebal following the victory at Ai forms a perfect continuity in the life of both Joshua and Israel. Their defeat and subsequent victory motivated them to go back to the "drawing board," back to God's basics. This is why we read—

> Joshua built an altar to the LORD, the God of Israel, in Mount Ebal, just as Moses the servant of the LORD had commanded the sons of Israel, as it is written in the book of the law of Moses, an altar of uncut stones, on which no man had wielded an iron tool; and they offered burnt offerings on it to the LORD, and sacrificed peace offerings. (Josh. 8:30–31)

Reviewing God's Laws

Not only had Moses instructed Israel to "build an altar to the Lord" at Mount Ebal, but also carefully to "review the law" in the hearing of all the people of Israel. Memories tended to fade, particularly in a primitive culture where there were no Bibles that could be read regularly. Effective learning depended on oral communication from spiritual leaders. And Moses' command to the people of Israel was that—once they had entered Canaan—they were to spend quality time at Mount Ebal reviewing God's laws (Deut. 27:1–3). Thus, we see Joshua doing what Moses commanded. First, he wrote the law on large stones (Josh. 8:32). Then "he read all the words of the law" (v. 34). We read: "There was not a word of all that Moses had commanded which Joshua did not read before all the assembly of Israel with the women and the little ones and the strangers who were living among them" (v. 35).

This was an explicit statement regarding Joshua's obedience to God's command in Joshua 1:8: "This book of the law *shall not depart from your mouth*, but you shall meditate on it day and night, so that you may be careful to do according to all that is written in it; for then you will make your way prosperous, and then you will have success."

A More Careful Look

This passage in Joshua 8:30–35, though very clearly a significant part of the flow of events of Israel's history, is skeletal in nature. This, it seems, is by design. The Holy Spirit was primarily concerned that we note clearly the contrast already referred to and the reasons why Joshua moved all of Israel to this unique place in Canaan to worship the Lord and to review His law.

What Actually Happened?

It's impossible to reconstruct all the specific details of this story from the historical record in Joshua 8. However, it's relatively simple to understand most of them when we go back and look at God's initial instruction to Israel through His servant Moses (Deut. 27).

Slabs for Writing

There were actually two events at Mount Ebal that involved "stones." Moses instructed the people of Israel to "set up . . . large stones." They were to "coat them with lime" and then to "write on them all the words of this law" (Deut. 27:2–3).[2] Subsequently, Joshua "wrote . . . a copy of the Law of Moses" on these stones (Josh. 8:32).

An Altar for Worship

The second set of stones formed the altar upon which the children of Israel offered burnt offerings and peace offerings (compare Deut. 27:5 and Josh. 8:30–31). These were stones that were taken from the earth in their natural state, evidently to make an altar that was not tainted by man's efforts at refinement. This altar was to reflect as much as possible God's creative hand—not man's. And it was on this altar that Israel made atonement for their sins according to God's law and also worshiped the God of Israel with offerings of thanksgiving and praise.[3]

Communicating God's Word

The most dramatic part of this story is the actual reading of the law of God to the people and their involvement in the process. Joshua's record gives a brief geographical setting for this event. "Half of them stood in front of Mount Gerizim and half of them in front of Mt. Ebal" (v. 33). But again the specific instructions in the Book of Deuteronomy fill in some unique details.

A Human Amplification System

Israel was actually camped in a valley between the two mountains—Ebal to the north and Gerizim to the south. Half of the tribes were camped closer to Ebal and half were camped closer to Gerizim. The Levitical priests were evidently camped in the lower part of the valley between the two mountains, where they placed the Ark of the Covenant. Though details are vague, it appears that Joshua first read a statement from the law. Then the priests repeated it in unison, serving as a human amplification system. As their voices echoed through the valley, all Israel responded to each statement by shouting back, "Amen."

A Sobering Message

What is more important than the method God used is the message He conveyed with this method. The means was indeed dramatic and sensational but the message was definite and sobering. Though what is recorded in Deuteronomy 27 is no doubt representative of what was read from the law, it contains sufficient information to reveal God's will regarding the kind of morality and ethics He demanded from His people. Nearly every significant relationship in life is represented in the twelve statements (Deut. 27:15–26).[4]

Though we do not have space to study carefully the nature of these twelve prohibitions recorded in Deuteronomy 27, a casual reading reveals the religious, moral and ethical deterioration that had taken place in the world of that day. This repre-sents a primary reason why God's hand of judgment fell on the Canaanites by means of His people Israel. And if Israel was to be victorious in their battles against "flesh and blood," it was imperative that they be victorious over "the rulers, against the powers, against the world forces of this darkness, against the spiritual forces of wickedness in the heavenly places" (Eph. 6:12).

A Profound Witness

Imagine, too, the impact this event had on all the Canaanites who lived in the vicinity of Mount Ebal and Gerizim. Like all the unique and dramatic situations in Israel's life, what happened would be repeated from one end of Canaan to the other.

Thus Israel paused in their march against the cities of Canaan both to nurture their personal relationship with God and to review His will for their lives. This in itself is one of the most important lessons that emerges from this passage for those of us who are Christians living in the twentieth-century world.

Becoming God's Man Today

Principles to Live By

Principle 1. We must take time on a consistent basis to maintain and regain perspective on God's will for our lives.

As with Israel, there are two aspects to this process.

Reviewing the Teachings of Scripture

We must consistently learn and review God's will through His Word. If we're not careful, we can get so busy—even "doing God's work"—that we fail to remember what the basics really are. Remember, the Scriptures are the only reliable and absolute source for discovering this kind of information.

Maintaining Our Relationship with God

We also must consistently nurture our personal relationship with God through worship and communion. This involves both the group process and personal meditation and prayer. In fact, it is almost impossible to develop a warm, meaningful relationship with the Lord if we are not developing warm, meaningful relationships with other members of the body of Christ. Thus, we need relationships with one another as well as a dynamic relationship with God in order to grow spiritually.

We do not have to offer sacrifices for our sins as Israel did. Jesus Christ became the supreme sacrifice once and for all (Heb. 10:4–10). But as Christians we are not to forsake "our own assembling together, as is the habit of some"; rather, we are "to stimulate one another to love and good deeds" (vv. 24–25).

We are to "continually offer up a sacrifice of praise to God, that is, the fruit of lips that give thanks to His name" (13:15).

Principle 2. God never promised that He will specifically reveal His will directly to us every time we need to make a decision.

There was a time when I didn't understand how to determine the will of God, particularly in areas where the Scriptures are silent. One reason is that I didn't understand the freedom God has given me to make decisions within the context of His written Word. God never promised to reveal His will directly to us every time we face a decision. Rather, He gives us sufficient information and principles from the Scriptures to help us make proper decisions at any moment in our lives. Furthermore, He has given us His Holy Spirit to guide us in interpreting the Scriptures.

This Was True in Old Testament Days

Even in the Old Testament era—a time when God frequently spoke by direct revelation—Joshua was responsible to review what God had *already* revealed to Moses. He was to meditate on the "book of the law." He was to study it and communicate it to Israel on a regular basis. This is why Joshua had his people meet together at Mount Ebal.

How Much More So Today

If this was true in Joshua's day, how much more so in our day when we have the full written revelation of God in the sixty-six books of the Bible. Too many Christians are relying on God to reveal Himself directly in the midst of the decision-making process, without realizing that they are responsible to seek His will through what He has already revealed.

Important Guidelines

How can we determine God's will for us today? There are four important considerations:

First, is there any statement in God's written revelation (the Bible) that is in opposition to this decision?

As Christians living in the twentieth century, we are privileged people. The children of Israel did not have access to the Word of God as we do. They were dependent solely upon spiritual leaders, such as Joshua and the priests, to communicate and review the law of God for them. By contrast, we have access to the Scriptures themselves.

How can the Scriptures help us in making decisions? For example, God makes it very clear in Scripture that a Christian should not marry a non-Christian. Also, He makes it clear that Christians should not be divorced simply because they are having difficulty with compatibility in some area in their lives. To do either of these would be a violation of His perfect will. There's no way to make Scripture conform to our feelings if our feelings are out of harmony with Scripture.

We must look, then, for direct exhortations in Scripture that will help us make decisions. The better we know the Word of God, the more we will be able to make right decisions.

Second, what do other mature Christians think about this decision? What advice can they give?

Mature Christians who know the Word of God and who are living spiritual lives are important in helping us determine God's will. That's why we must never forsake the assembling of ourselves together with other Christians. Often through the functioning body of Christ we learn what His will is for our lives.

What other people think—even mature Christians—is not as important as our personal knowledge of Scripture. Nor can they make decisions for us where the Scriptures are silent. However, there is safety in a "multitude of counselors" (Prov. 11:14). Corporate wisdom from godly people is significant in God's scheme of things (Eph. 4:16).

Third, what circumstances point to the fact that this may be a right or wrong decision?

Circumstances *are* important in the decision-making process. However, we must be careful that we do not allow negative circumstances to be the *primary* factor in making a decision for or against a matter. Many times Christians are called upon to circumvent negative circumstances and to break through environmental barriers. The fact that a Christian is having struggles because of negative circumstances does not mean he is out of the will of God in pursuing a particular course of action. It's at this point that wise counselors play an important role in our lives.

Fourth, how do I feel about this decision?

Feelings should be considered last. They are important, but they also can be deceptive. Negative emotions may represent purely psychological struggles. Any difficult decision creates anxious if not painful feelings. Imagine what would have happened if Jesus had paid attention to His feelings when He was praying in the Garden? In His humanity, He wanted to walk away from the cross. But in spite of His strong negative emotions, He did the will of God.

On the other hand, positive emotions may simply mean this is something *we* want to do! This is why feelings must always be tested and evaluated by what God says in His Word.

Points of Action

Read the following questions and circle the answer that best represents your behavior.

1. Am I taking time out of my busy schedule to review God's will for my life? *(Never) (Sometimes) (Always)*

2. Is it part of my priority system to include regular Bible reading and Bible study, both with other Christians and by myself? *(Never) (Sometimes) (Always)*

3. Am I taking advantage of opportunities God has given me to discover His will for my life through personal and group Bible study? *(Never) (Sometimes) (Always)*

4. Am I pausing sufficiently in my busy schedule to meet regularly with Christ's body in order to develop meaningful relationships with other Christians and with the Lord? *(Never) (Sometimes) (Always)*

5. Do I pause sufficiently— even in doing God's work—to thank God and praise Him for who He is and what He is doing for me? *(Never) (Sometimes) (Always)*

6. To what extent am I trying to determine God's will through existential experience rather than through His written Word? *(Never) (Sometimes) (Always)*

A Man's Man Is a Godly Man

Reread the above questions under Points of Action. Note particularly the numbers you have selected to indicate your response to these questions. As you do, ask the Holy Spirit to impress on your heart one lesson you need to apply more effectively in your life. Then write out a specific goal. For example, you may not be taking time out of your busy schedule to meet regularly with Christ's body in order to develop meaningful relationships with other Christians and with the Lord. Even if you circled number 4 which indicates that you do this "sometimes," this probably is a particular need in your life.

Set a Goal

With God's help, I will begin immediately to carry out the following goal in my life:

_____

_____

_____

Memorize the Following Scripture

> *Trust in the Lord with all your heart, and do not lean on your own understanding. In all your ways acknowledge Him, and He will make your paths straight.*
> PROVERBS 3:5–6

Chapter 11

Caught Off Guard
Read Joshua 9:3–27

*I*f you're like I am, the times when you are most vulnerable to making errors in judgment come at moments when you least expect them to happen. Ironically, my greatest mistakes occur at the end of a rather successful time of ministry and when I'm most aware of God's will for my life. If we let our guard down at all during those moments, Satan will surely find the chink in our armor.

Make no mistake about it! Satan is a subtle enemy. If he cannot reach his insidious goals by causing us flagrantly to disobey the Word of God, on occasions he will appear as an "angel of light" and actually use God's truth to trip us.

He did this to Joshua, and, unfortunately, this Old Testament leader made a decision that was irreversible.

Reflect for a Moment

Joshua had faced the defeat at Ai with unusual courage. As difficult as it had been, he had dealt with Achan's sin. Furthermore, he had built an altar to the Lord and "offered burnt offerings" and "peace offerings" to the Lord at Mount Ebal and Mount Gerizim. All Israel had acknowledged God and worshiped Him as their protector and provider.

Joshua also reviewed the law of God for all Israel. He took them back to basics. He carefully copied on stones everything God had revealed to Moses. He then read the law in the presence of all Israel (8:35).

Everything seemed to be in order for Joshua and Israel to move forward victoriously. They had learned their lessons well! If they simply obeyed God in all things, they would never repeat their "Ai experience."

Meanwhile, throughout Canaan

While Israel was worshiping the Lord and reviewing God's laws, the kings of Canaan rallied to form an alliance against God's people. Knowing that Ai had at first succeeded in routing Israel may have given them a ray of hope. Obviously, they didn't understand the supernatural factors at work in both Israel's initial defeat and subsequent victory. Unfortunately, they concluded that what they needed were more men and more swords and spears.

From a human perspective, their thinking made sense, since Ai had defeated Israel when Joshua had initially sent a small contingent of men (7:3–4). But from God's perspective, it made no sense at all. In their arrogance and spiritual blindness, these kings totally disregarded what had happened at Jericho—and throughout Israel's journey from Egypt to Canaan. How could they forget the miracle at Jordan?

Not Everyone Agreed

Among those represented in this summit meeting were men from Gibeon who were called Hivites (9:1, 7). Gibeon was one of the largest cities in Canaan. Though the people of Gibeon didn't have a king, their city was just as respected as any other city in Canaan. We read that Gibeon was "a great city, like one of the royal cities." In fact, "it was greater than Ai, and all its men were mighty" (10:2).

A Minority Decision

Though all of the kings who gathered to form this military alliance agreed that they would stick together in their fight against Joshua and Israel (9:2), the Gibeonites decided on another course of action. As they listened to the kings discuss Israel's victory over Jericho and Ai, they came to a different conclusion (v. 3). Rather than join in this military alliance against Israel, they decided they would come up with a strategy to make peace, not war.

The Gibeonite Deception

The Gibeonites were cunning. They knew they could never defeat Israel in war—no matter how many men the alliance could muster. They understood clearly that Israel's military resources were supernatural. They refused to ignore what had happened in previous battles. Any military strategist who was objective at all would be forced to conclude that Israel's exploits were divinely directed.

In a Multitude of Counselors

Why did the Gibeonites refuse to join the kings of Canaan in their military alliance? Why was their conclusion different regarding Israel's capabilities? Personally I believe their response had something to do with their form of government. As far as we know, they were the only people in Canaan who had a republic. Rather than being ruled by a sovereign king, a body of elders who represented the people governed the city. Obviously, they had a leader among leaders, but their decisions were based on input from many people—which no doubt led them to the conclusion that they would be foolhardy to try to defeat Israel, even if all the other cities in Canaan joined in the attack.

Their conclusion was accurate. But unfortunately, their strategy was deceptive. Had they been willing to forsake their gods and follow the God of Abraham, Isaac and Jacob, the Lord would have withdrawn His hand of judgment, even if they were Canaanites. Rahab and her household illustrate this fact dramatically. But the Gibeonites did not allow their *accurate knowledge* to lead them to *proper actions*.

A Shrewd Strategy

The Gibeonites deceived Israel by giving the impression that they had come from a far country, *outside* the land of Canaan. They put on shabby clothes and sandals that appeared to be worn out from a long journey. They "took worn-out sacks on their donkeys, and wineskins, worn-out and torn and mended . . . and all the bread of their provision was dry and had become crumbled" (vv. 4–5). And when they arrived in Israel's camp—after traveling no more than ten or twenty miles—"they went to Joshua . . . and said to him and to the men of Israel, 'We have come from a far country; now therefore, make a covenant with us'" (v. 6).

A Brilliant Maneuver

From a human point of view, this was a brilliant strategy. It reveals that the Gibeonite leaders had a thorough knowledge of God's instructions to Israel long before they ever entered the land of Canaan. They actually used this knowledge to deceive Israel. What was this knowledge? All Canaanites were to be destroyed or driven out.

Many years before, God had said to Moses:

"And I will fix your boundary from the Red Sea to the sea of the Philistines, and from the wilderness to the River Euphrates; for I will deliver the inhabitants of the land into your hand, and you will drive them out before you. *You shall make no covenant with them or with their gods.* They shall not live in your land, lest they make you sin against Me; for if

you serve their gods, it will surely be a snare to you."
(Exod. 23:31–33)

Provision for People Outside of Canaan

The Gibeonites knew what God had said to Israel—that no city
in Canaan was to be spared. But they also knew that God had
made provisions to spare cities *outside* of Canaan. Moses made
this clear when he reviewed the law for Israel following their
forty-year experience in the wilderness:

> "When you approach a city to fight against it, you shall
> offer it terms of peace. And it shall come about, if it agrees
> to make peace with you and opens to you, then it shall be
> that *all the people who are found in it shall become your forced
> labor and shall serve you.* However, if it does not make peace
> with you, but makes war against you, then you shall besiege
> it." (Deut. 20:10–12)

This is why they wanted to appear as if they had come from
a "far country." They also knew they had to make the first move.
They did not have the option to wait for Israel to approach them
since they were Canaanites and had already come under God's
judgment. Their solution was to try to convince Israel that they
had come from a distant place outside the land of Canaan.

They Had Done Their Homework Well

Note also that the Gibeonite contingency avoided any reference to Jericho and Ai when they first approached Joshua:

> "Your servants have come from a *very far country* because of
> the fame of the LORD your God; for we have heard the report
> of Him and all that He did in Egypt, and all that He did to
> the two kings of the Amorites who were beyond the Jordan,
> to Sihon king of Heshbon and to Og king of Bashan who
> was at Ashtaroth." (Josh. 9:9–10)

A Perfect Plan

Everything fit together perfectly. They had done their research well. In fact, they knew so much about Israel and their laws that it appears some of the people from Gibeon may have been "listening in" when Joshua reviewed the law of God at Mount Ebal and Mount Gerizim. They probably did, since they actually used God's instructions to Israel to reach their personal goals. They volunteered to be servants. They avoided any reference to Canaanite cities—to give the impression they knew nothing of this land. Their clothes and their provisions were worn-out and appeared to be aged from traveling a long distance. And perhaps most impressive and deceptive, they acknowledged the God of Israel.

Caught Off Guard

The Gibeonite strategy worked. Joshua was caught off guard. Impressed with all the evidence, he "made peace with them and made a covenant with them" (v. 15).

Unfortunately, Joshua made this decision without seeking "the counsel of the LORD" (v. 14). You see, there was another divine source God had given Israel for just such occasions. He could have gone to the high priest to seek God's will directly (Num. 27:18–21). But he didn't. Even though he had been skeptical earlier in his encounter with the Gibeonites (Josh. 9:7), he responded too quickly. He was convinced that these people were telling him the truth. He was also deceived.

A Great Strength—a Great Weakness!

"How could this have happened?" you ask. The facts are it can happen to anyone—especially to a man like Joshua. Though he was a great leader, his greatest strength became a great weakness. He found it easy to trust people. Because he was an honest man with pure motives, he viewed others—even his enemies—through his own eyes. He probably found it difficult to ask the really tough questions.

Joshua was even acting as God had said he should in circumstances such as this seemed to be. The problem was that the circumstances were not as Joshua thought. Consequently, he misapplied the Scriptures. He didn't have all the facts.

Does this mean God doesn't want us to trust others? Not at all! But Joshua's experience teaches us to be cautious, since things are not always as they appear. Though we are certainly not to go through life "looking" for deceit in others, we must realize that some people *will* be dishonest in order to protect themselves and to meet their own needs.

A Personal Experience

As a pastor, this has happened to me on a number of occasions. I've often been approached by people—outside the church usually—who try to take advantage of me and our congregation. They are looking for a handout.

In most instances, their "sad stories" are quite believable. And since the Bible teaches we are to help people in need, it's easy to avoid asking the tough questions and to act too quickly.

Frankly, it's something I've had to develop, since I am really a "soft touch" when it comes to meeting people's needs. Though difficult—and after having made some bad judgments—I've learned to ask the really tough questions.

I remember a couple that walked into the church office and unfolded a tale of woe. Their car had blown an engine and they needed to get from Dallas to Denver. They asked for money to fix their car. They had approached me, they said, since they had heard that *our church* was a caring church. They also assured me they would repay the money once they got back home—especially since he had a good job.

I was cordial but asked for some identification—including the name of his employer and a phone number. I offered to call—at our expense—to see if I could arrange to have some money wired to Dallas. At that moment, they began to rant and rave and to accuse me of "not being a Christian." I held my ground, however, and they stomped out of the office using some words that are not printable. Though difficult for me, I was obviously asking the right questions!

Egg on His Face

Ironically, it took only three days for Joshua to discover his mistake (9:16). Imagine his surprise and chagrin when he heard that these people were neighbors.

In order to make sure what they had heard was not a rumor—and to save face—a group made the three-day journey to Gibeon, the central location. What they discovered was embarrassing. They formed three smaller suburban locations called Chephirah, Beeroth and Kiriath-jearim (v. 17).

It Was No Rumor

Joshua had been terribly deceived—along with a number of other men in Israel. Unfortunately, it was a decision they could not reverse. They had made a covenant with them in the name of "the Lord the God of Israel." Even though Joshua's mistake was based on false information, it was a decision that involved God—His name and His reputation.

Two Wrongs Never Make a Right

If the children of Israel had broken their oath with the Gibeonites, they would have brought the name of the God of Israel into contempt among the Canaanites. Though Joshua and all Israel definitely sinned in allowing themselves to be deceived, to break the covenant would have compounded the sin.

I am reminded of another experience I had as a pastor. A man approached me one day between services. I was on the platform getting things in order. As he approached me, he called me by my first name and asked if he could speak with me for a moment.

Frankly, I didn't recognize the man. But, he talked to me *as if I should know him*. In fact, he was prepared for my hesitant response (he could see it on my face) and said—"You know me. I live just down the street and have been attending the church."

Feeling embarrassed that I didn't know who he was, I went along with his scheme. He asked me for money to get a plane ticket to Tucson, Arizona. His wife, he said, went to visit her ill mother who was in the hospital. However, as she was driving to the hospital, his wife had a car accident and she ended up in the same hospital. He informed me he had just found out about it and needed a plane ticket to get to Tucson. He needed an additional fifty dollars to buy the ticket.

Deeply moved by his story—and embarrassed to ask some difficult questions—I went over to one of our men who had the cash. I immediately borrowed the money and gave it to "the stranger" and he left the sanctuary. As soon as he walked out the door, I knew instinctively that I had made a bad judgment!

In reconstructing the story, this man saw my name on the sign in front of the church. Since we wear name tags, he approached another man in the parking lot, called him by name, and asked if he knew where I was—also calling me by my first name. He discovered I was in the sanctuary and the rest of the story is history. Though my mistake was certainly not as great as Joshua's, I definitely had "egg on my face" too!

A Catch 22

What was Joshua to do? He had violated the will of God by making a covenant with the Gibeonites. When he discovered his mistake, he took action. He immediately demanded an explanation. "'Why have you deceived us?'" he asked (v. 22).

When Joshua discovered what had happened, he knew he couldn't reverse his decision. He could do only one thing—

pronounce a curse of servanthood on the Gibeonites. "'You shall never cease being slaves,'" he said (v. 23).

It's Better to Serve and Live

The Gibeonites were actually pleased with Joshua's decision. They would rather serve Israel and *live* than fight Israel and *die*. "'We are in your hands,'" they responded to Joshua's indictment. "'Do as it seems good and right in your sight to do to us'" (v. 25).

Though God had originally specified that the Gibeonites were to be put to death or driven out of Canaan, He honored Joshua's covenant to preserve them. Since His name was involved, He would not go back on His promise. God would demonstrate this commitment several times over the years on behalf of these people.

Another Painful Lesson

Israel was called upon to honor the covenant with the Gibeonites soon after the agreement had been made. Five kings of the Amorites, angered and threatened by the Gibeonite strategy, decided to attack the Gibeonite cities (10:3–4).

The Gibeonites quickly sent word to Joshua asking for help. And Israel, because these people were now their servants, acted immediately—and with God's blessing.

In fact, on this occasion Joshua evidently sought the Lord's direct will through the high priest, for we read: "And the Lord said to Joshua, 'Do not fear them, for I have given them into your hands; not one of them shall stand before you'" (v. 8). Again, Joshua had learned a very valuable but painful lesson.

Becoming God's Man Today

Principles to Live By

Principle 1. Christians can be led astray by making superficial judgments based upon the Word of God.

Remember that Joshua had just reviewed the complete law for Israel. They had spent days and perhaps weeks at Mount Ebal and Mount Gerizim. No doubt God's statements that Israel could make a covenant with people outside of Canaan but not within Canaan were freshly embedded in Joshua's mind. It was at this very point that Satan attacked this man of God and the other leaders in Israel and deceived them.

Lying Is One of Satan's Tactics

Satan *is* a subtle enemy, and lying is one of his common tactics. Jesus called him "the father of lies." Furthermore, one of his most deceptive tactics is to use God's Word to achieve his insidious goals.

Satan attempted to lead Jesus Christ astray with this same strategy when he tempted Him in the wilderness. Taking Him to the pinnacle of the Temple, he said to Jesus, "If You are the Son of God throw Yourself down" and then, he said, *"for it is written,* 'He will give His angels charge concerning You; and on their hands they will bear You up, lest You strike Your foot against a stone'" (Matt. 4:6).

Jesus Christ was not deceived as Joshua was. He never was, because He was the divine Son of God. In this case He reciprocated with the Word of God, rightly interpreted and correctly spoken, to counter Satan. Jesus replied—"It is written again, 'You shall not tempt the Lord your God'" (Matt. 4:7, NKJV).

Avoiding Deception Today

How can every Christian man—and all Christians—fall prey to this kind of satanic tactic? More importantly, how can we avoid this kind of deception?

Principle 2. We can be deceived if we use the Bible mystically.

There are some Christians who take a very superficial and mystical approach in using the Word of God to determine God's will for their lives. For example, they allow the Bible to fall open, trusting that the first verse that meets their eyes will be God's specific word to help them make a particular decision.

God can certainly use this method, but it has many inherent dangers. There is sufficient evidence that sincere Christians have been led astray by using the Bible so superficially.

I remember a story about a man who was seeking God's will for his life. He let the Bible fall open and his eyes fell on the text where Judas went out and hung himself. Jolted by what he read, he tried again. This time the Bible fell open and his eyes fell on Jesus' words—"Go and do likewise!" Obviously, this man learned a valuable lesson. This is not a good method for determining God's will. All of us must understand the totality of Scripture. Furthermore, we must understand it in its proper context. However, this leads to another important principle.

Principle 3. We can be deceived if we read and study the Bible subjectively and without good principles of interpretation.

This mistake in using the Bible to determine God's will is closely related to the one just described. However, the second mistake involves a more serious use of the Scriptures. In this instance, we often want to substantiate or prove a predetermined set of beliefs or desires.

Actually, it's possible to make the Bible teach almost anything if we ignore the basic principles of literary interpretation. This approach to Bible study has led to all kinds of erroneous systems of theology, which in turn have created a number of cults and isms that deny the total truth of Scripture.

To understand the Bible and what God is actually saying to us today, we must remember to use at least three basic guidelines:

First, determine what the words, phrases, and sentences of Scripture actually mean in context.

Second, discover what insights you can gain from the historical and cultural setting in which the Scriptures were written. In other words, what was the original meaning of scriptural statements?

Third, discern what grammatical, historical, cultural, and literary reasons there may be for taking an approach other than that which is literal.

Some people believe the Bible is purely allegorical and figurative, rather than a historical document. Authors of Scripture certainly used allegory and figurative language—like other writers—but they used this approach to illustrate literal meaning. To misunderstand this normal way of interpreting Scripture can lead to all kinds of false conclusions.

Principle 4. We can be deceived if we bring circumstances to bear on Scripture rather than evaluating circumstances in the light of Scripture.

Circumstantial factors are important in determining God's will. This we pointed out in a previous chapter (see pp. 139–40). However, we must never allow circumstances to be the primary factor in determining the Lord's will. Circumstances can be deceptive, as they were in Joshua's encounter with the Gibeonites. Everything looked right to Joshua. Furthermore, God had even spoken regarding what to do in this kind of situation. The problem was that circumstances were not as they appeared!

It is at this point that Satan may strike the hardest. Since we live in a world of time and space, we become accustomed to evaluating events in the light of our circumstances. Consequently, Satan makes use of our natural tendencies, our cultural understanding, and our psychological makeup.

To complicate matters, the line between making a correct decision and a bad one may be fine. Had Joshua simply asked more questions, waited just a day or so, and evaluated the total situation more carefully, he would have discovered the deception before he made that final, irreversible decision.

Fortunately, most of our mistakes are reversible. Even in Joshua's case, he picked up the pieces and did what he could to correct the situation without committing a second sin to try to undo the first one. In Christ, there is always hope, no matter what our past mistakes.

Points of Action

The fact that we have the Bible to guide us in making decisions is a great blessing. But we must make sure we use it correctly. Check yourself. Circle the answer that best describes your response. How often do you violate the following guidelines in your use of the Bible:

1. I tend to use the Bible mystically, in reality a "spiritual chance" method in determining what God's will is for me personally. *(Never) (Sometimes) (Always)*

2. I tend to read and study the Bible subjectively, violating basic principles of Bible interpretation.
   (Never) (Sometimes) (Always)

3. I tend to allow circumstances to take precedence over God's Word in determining His will for my life.
   (Never) (Sometimes) (Always)

A Man's Man Is a Godly Man

Reread the statements under Points of Action. While you are doing this, ask the Holy Spirit to impress on your heart one lesson you need to apply more effectively in your life. Then write out a specific goal suggested by that lesson. For example, the number you circled may indicate that you allow circumstances to take precedence over God's Word in determining His will for your life.

Set a Goal

With God's help, I will begin immediately to carry out the following goal in my life:

_____

_____

_____

Memorize the Following Scripture

For even Satan disguises himself as an angel of light. Therefore it is not surprising if his servants also disguise themselves as servants of righteousness; whose end shall be according to their deeds.
2 CORINTHIANS 11:14–15

Chapter 12

God Will Not Forget You

Read Joshua 14:6–15

A difficult thing for many of us is to be faithful when we're not in a prominent position. Somehow we function better when others know how well we're doing. This is a natural tendency. But the true test of our commitment to Jesus Christ is how well we function when we have to operate behind the scenes, even making it possible for someone else to be in the limelight.

A "Behind the Scenes" Man

Caleb illustrates this kind of commitment as no other Bible character. Though the Bible says little about him compared with Joshua, what is written reflects a man who was Joshua's spiritual equal. In fact, in some respects, he excelled Joshua as a leader. But once God appointed Joshua as Moses' successor, Caleb stood quietly beside Joshua—often behind the scenes doing God's will in supporting the Lord's chosen leader of Israel.

Victory after Victory

Following Joshua's treaty with the Gibeonites, the events leading to the division of the land among the tribes of Israel are recorded in rapid succession (see the following map).[1]

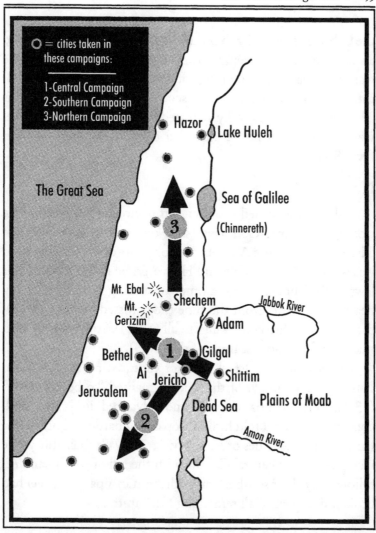

The map legend reads:

○ = cities taken in these campaigns:

1-Central Campaign
2-Southern Campaign
3-Northern Campaign

Hazor
Lake Huleh
The Great Sea
Sea of Galilee
(Chinnereth)
Mt. Ebal
Mt. Gerizim
Shechem
Jabbok River
Adam
Bethel
Gilgal
Ai
Jericho
Shittim
Jerusalem
Dead Sea
Plains of Moab
Amon River

Joshua's Three Campaigns

Southern Canaan

The kings in southern Canaan were greatly threatened by the Gibeonites' alliance with Israel (10:1–5). Five of these men rallied their forces together and their first move was to attack the Gibeonites in order to punish them for joining Israel—and also to keep Israel's strength from expanding even further. The war was a fiasco for the kings of the south. Israel, because of the covenant, came to the rescue of the Gibeonites. This alliance not only soundly defeated the five kings, but Israel went on to defeat numerous other cities in southern Canaan (vv. 28–43).

Northern Canaan

Joshua next turned his attention to northern Canaan. The story is the same. God gave Israel one victory after another. There were no more Ai's and no more improper alliances. God was with Israel just as He said He would be if they obeyed His laws (1:8). Though it was a time-consuming process involving nearly seven years from the time they crossed Jordan (11:18), they defeated thirty-one kings in all (12:24). And then we read that "the land had rest from war" (11:23).

Understand that Israel had not captured all the Promised Land. In fact, "much of the land" remained "to be possessed" (13:1). But "Joshua was old and advanced in years," and, consequently, God told him to stop doing battle and divide the land among the tribes of Israel (vv. 1, 7). With their thirty-one victories, first in central Canaan with the fall of Jericho and Ai, followed by their southern and northern campaigns, Israel had broken the spirit of all remaining Canaanites.

God's Future Plan

Once the land was divided among the tribes, each individual tribe was responsible to complete the task. With a few exceptions, Israel had been faithful to God and they were now entitled to their inheritance. And if they continued to obey the Lord, little by little they would be able to possess all the land God had promised them (see the map on the following page).

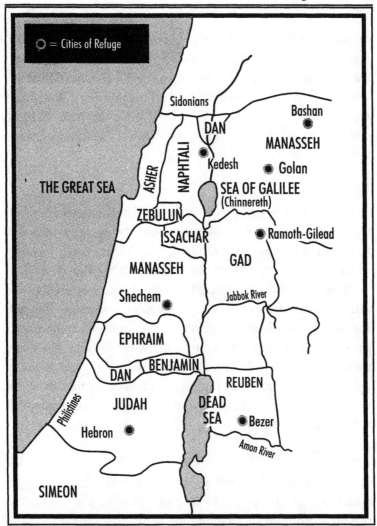

Canaan and the Twelve Tribes

Caleb Walks on Stage

At this point in the history of Israel, we once again encounter Caleb. Though he was eighty-five years old, and though he had faithfully and patiently served God in Joshua's shadow, his memory had not faded nor had his physical abilities diminished. He remembered a promise God had made to him forty-five years earlier and he knew this was the day to refresh Joshua's memory. This he did with a very specific reminder: "'You know the word which the LORD spoke to Moses the man of God concerning you and me in Kadesh–barnea,'" he said to Joshua (14:6).

Reflections

Forty-five years earlier, long before Israel entered Canaan, God issued an order to Moses to send twelve spies into the land—a man for each tribe. Along with Joshua, Caleb was one of those men, representing the tribe of Judah (Num. 13:6, 8).

When the spies completed their task and returned to the camp of Israel, ten spies brought back a negative report. Though they acknowledged that the land flowed "with milk and honey," they also reported it was a land filled with fortified cities and strong warriors (vv. 27–29, 32–33). "'We are not able to go up against the people,'" they reported, "'for they are too strong for us'" (v. 31). Fear begets fear and this negative report frightened the children of Israel.

Caleb's Bold Stand

In the midst of growing pessimism, Caleb dared to disagree with the majority report. With great boldness and confidence in God's promises he "quieted the people before Moses," and shouted for all to hear—"'We should by all means go up and take possession of it, for we shall surely overcome it'" (v. 30).

At this moment, Joshua was silent. He agreed with Caleb, but remained in the background. Caleb was the spokesman!

In his earlier years, Joshua seemed to be reserved and in some instances a very fearful man, particularly when faced with leadership responsibility. Caleb was courageous, bolder and more willing to face threatening situations head-on.

All of Us Get Intimidated

All of us at times need someone who is stronger than we are. I remember when I was a young administrator at Moody Bible Institute in Chicago. I had oversight of the Evening School, a wonderful opportunity to minister to nearly one thousand lay people from all over the Chicago area. However, at times I became intimidated in view of what was to me an awesome task—particularly at my age. I was still in my late twenties.

However, I knew a Christian businessman who officed in downtown Chicago. He was a strong, dynamic individual who always seemed to be in control of life's challenges. Consequently, I periodically had lunch with Jerry—particularly when I was feeling insecure. And every time I returned to my office, I did so with a greater sense of inner strength, confidence, and vision. I drew strength from Jerry.

Joshua's Growing Courage

Joshua apparently drew strength from Caleb's courageous behavior. When the fear generated by the spies evolved into anger and rebellion against Moses, Joshua took a stand with Caleb and challenged Israel to claim God's promises and then to act on those promises. Tearing their clothes, they cried out:

> "If the LORD is pleased with us, then He will bring us into this land, and give it to us . . . only do not rebel against the LORD; and do not fear the people of the land, for they shall be our prey. Their protection has been removed from them, and the LORD is with us; do not fear them." (Num. 14:8–9)

Facing a Life-Threatening Situation

Unfortunately, Caleb's and Joshua's exhortations and warnings went unheeded. The children of Israel threatened to stone them.

Israel's rebellion brought God's anger and wrath on Israel. Initially the Lord was going to destroy his people, right there and then. However, Moses intervened and succeeded in persuading the Lord to spare their lives.

Once again God relented, but not without partial judgment. Because of their unbelief and failure to obey Him, God pronounced that all of that adult generation would never see the land. They would have to wander in the wilderness for forty years until they died. Only their children would be able to enter Canaan.

But there were two exceptions—Joshua and Caleb (v. 38). Because of their willingness to obey God, they would not die in the wilderness. They would be able to enter the land of Canaan.

God's Promise to Caleb

Originally God singled out Caleb for this special blessing:

> "Surely all the men . . . shall by no means see the land . . . But My servant Caleb, because he has had a different spirit and has *followed Me fully*, I will bring into the land which he entered, and his descendants shall take possession of it." (vv. 22–24)

Why isn't Joshua's name mentioned? Apparently, God was honoring Caleb for his initial courage and boldness. Joshua's time would come, but at this moment, God wanted all to know that He would not forget Caleb. He was going to give him a special inheritance because he had *followed the Lord fully* (Num. 14:14; Deut. 1:36).

When God instructed Joshua to divide the land among the tribes, Caleb stepped out of the shadows and walked onto God's great stage. He had waited forty-five years for this moment. He remembered God's promise as if it were yesterday. Thus he reminded Joshua:

> "I was forty years old when Moses the servant of the LORD sent me from Kadesh-barnea to spy out the land, and I brought word back to him as it was in my heart. Nevertheless my brethren who went up with me made the heart of the

people melt with fear; but *I followed the* LORD *my God fully.*" (Josh. 14:7–8).

A Specific Inheritance

Though the biblical record in Numbers and Deuteronomy makes no reference to a specific inheritance for Caleb (only a general reference to the inheritance of the land), God must have mentioned at that time the exact area Caleb spied out in Canaan. Consequently, Caleb also reminded Joshua of Moses' response at that time to God's promise: "So Moses swore on that day, saying, 'Surely the land on which your foot has trodden shall be an inheritance to you and to your children forever, because you have *followed the* LORD *my God fully*'" (v. 9).

Caleb's Specific Request

At age eighty-five and after supporting Joshua for seven war-filled years, he boldly and courageously asked for the "hill country about which the LORD spoke on that day" (v. 12). This specific request confirms the fact that the Lord had spelled out clearly that He would give Caleb a special place in Canaan because of his faithfulness.

The "Hill Country"

This was the exact area Caleb spied out many years before. And though it was strongly fortified and heavily populated by men of great size, God promised Caleb he would be able to defeat his enemies, even in his old age. Caleb was as confident of God's promise as he was in himself and his own abilities.

Age Eighty-five—And Going Strong

"I am still as strong today as I was in the day Moses sent me; as my strength was then, so my strength is now, for war and for going out and coming in. . . . Perhaps the LORD will be

with me, and I shall drive them out as the LORD has spoken."
(vv. 11–12)

Here again we have that unique and intricate balance between God—confidence and self-confidence. And it should be noted that Caleb's use of the word "perhaps" does not imply doubt, but humility. Caleb knew he could win the battle. If he believed it when they were still in the wilderness forty-five years before, how much more so after having seen God deliver thirty-one Canaanite kings into their hands.

Caleb's Special Reward

Joshua remembered! How could he forget? He immediately blessed Caleb and gave him the land God had promised him for an inheritance. Perhaps his response went something like this: "Caleb, it's yours. You deserve it. I'm sorry I forgot! It's because of you that I mustered enough courage to take a stand against Israel's hostility and disobedience. It was because of you that I spoke out against their rebellion and unbelief. You helped me become the man that I am—a man that God could trust to lead Israel in place of Moses. I drew strength from you, Caleb. And you have been faithful to me. You've supported me, helped me, encouraged me. You've never shown jealousy or resentment because you were not chosen to lead Israel, even though you were a stronger man than I, both physically and psychologically. I'm sorry I didn't remember God's promise myself. I'm glad you reminded me! It's yours! Take the mountain God promised you."

Becoming God's Man Today

Principles to Live By

Following are five very significant observations regarding Caleb's life, which in turn lead to five practical lessons for every Christian man.

Principle 1. God honors men who walk in His will.

Three times in this chapter, we read that God's blessing on Caleb was based on the fact that he had followed the Lord fully. God honored his faithful obedience to His commands.

God wants us to be obedient to all that He asks us to do. Note however that the disobedience of Israel interfered with Caleb's desire to go into the land. Yet God viewed his true *willingness to obey* as actual obedience.

The same is true for you and me. There are times when other people in our lives limit our ability to be as responsive to the will of God as we'd like to be. However, God knows our hearts, just as He did Caleb's.

For example, I know men who are married to women who are either unbelievers or very carnal. These men have a desire to serve Jesus Christ more fully with their talents, their time, and their treasures. However, they are limited in what they can do because of the disunity and hostility it would create. Again, God understands those situations and honors our heart response.

Group Disobedience

Sometimes we find our personal obedience lacking because of group disobedience—perhaps in our church or business. In situations where the circumstances are beyond our control, God also looks at our hearts and what *we* do in the situation. Caleb was willing to take a stand for God's Word even though he knew he would be rejected by his own people. What about you?

Be Careful

Christians must make sure they are taking a stand for God's Word and not for their own prejudiced opinions. Some Christians suffer needlessly because of a lack of knowledge of God's Word. In Caleb's case there was no question. Israel was in direct violation of God's command. In this situation, Caleb would not compromise his convictions.

Principle 2. God honors men who take a stand against the majority when the majority is wrong.

Caleb's obedience was in the context of a minority report. The vote was ten to two in favor of disobedience.

How easy it is to side with the majority; to compromise our Christian convictions; to operate out of fear. Not so with Caleb. Even when Joshua appears to have been afraid to speak up, Caleb spoke out boldly. What about you?

Principle 3. God honors men who take a stand for Him even though it means rejection by the group.

Caleb's obedience was in the context of group rejection. The people literally wanted to stone him. Most of us have never had our lives threatened because of our stand for God's Word. However, it's easy to be inhibited and fearful even in the midst of minor rejections from those who do not want to follow God.

The apostle Paul stands out as a dynamic example for all of us in this respect. "For I am not ashamed of the gospel," he wrote to the Romans, "for it is the power of God for salvation to everyone who believes, to the Jew first and also to the Greek" (Rom. 1:16). And when he knew he was going to stand before the Roman emperor, perhaps to face the death penalty, he wrote to his faithful prayer supporters in Philippi:

> For I know that this shall turn out for my deliverance through your prayers and the provision of the Spirit of Jesus Christ, according to my earnest expectation and hope, that I shall not be put to shame in anything, but that with all boldness, Christ shall even now, as always, be exalted in my body, whether by life or by death. (Phil. 1:19–20)

Principle 4. God honors men who faithfully follow Him.

Caleb had been obedient for forty-five years, even though Joshua was the man God chose to lead the children of Israel into the land. How easy it is to become jealous and resentful when other Christians receive more attention than we do—especially when we feel we deserve it as much as they. To be faithful behind the scenes is difficult, but it's a true test of character. Remember, too, that God often tests us to see how faithful we are under these circumstances. If we pass the test, He then is able to entrust us with greater responsibility.

Principle 5. God will not forget men who serve Him faithfully and consistently.

Caleb's obedience was eventually honored and rewarded, even though it was forty-five years later. God did not forget His promise to Caleb. He always honors faithful obedience.

Remember that God never forgets. Eventually He will reward us for faithful obedience. Like Caleb, some of that reward often comes in this life, but it will definitely come in eternity. And of course, eternal rewards are those that really count.

Points of Action

Ask God to help you become a faithful and obedient Christian—to "follow the Lord fully" in all He says, no matter what the consequences. Write out a personal and specific goal that you want to carry out immediately—this week. Pray for God's help. Remember the words of Paul who said, "I can do all things through Him who strengthens me" (Phil. 4:13).

1. How obedient am I to all that God commands?
   (Never) (Sometimes) (Always)

2. When the majority wants to do what is wrong in the sight of God, do I take a stand for what is right?
   (Never) (Sometimes) (Always)

3. When I am faced with group rejection because I want to obey the Word of God, do I take a stand for what I know to be the will of God? *(Never) (Sometimes) (Always)*

4. How faithful am I in my service to the Lord and to others when I have to work behind the scenes?
   (Never) (Sometimes) (Always)

5. Am I willing to wait patiently for God to fulfill His promises to me? *(Never) (Sometimes) (Always)*

A Man's Man Is a Godly Man

Reread the questions under Points of Action. As you do, ask the Holy Spirit to impress on your heart one lesson you need to apply more effectively in your life. Then write out a specific goal. For example, you may have a problem with feelings of rejection, particularly when you want to be obedient to the Word of God and the group wants to do something else. You know you need to take a stand for what you know to be the will of God.

Set a Goal

With God's help, I will begin immediately to carry out the following goal in my life:

_____

_____

_____

_____

Memorize the Following Scripture

Finally, be strong in the Lord, and in the strength of His might. Put on the full armor of God, that you may be able to stand firm against the schemes of the devil.
EPHESIANS 6:10–11

Chapter 13

A Man of God Speaks
Read Joshua 23:1–24:33

One thing that has made a profound impression on my life is that I have observed men whom God has mightily used get sidetracked in their later years. This observation applies not only to Christians who work and serve in a secular environment but to evangelists, pastors, and missionaries who serve in what we call full-time Christian ministry.

The Bible is filled with illustrations of men who failed God miserably—Solomon, for instance, and David, his father. Even God's great servant Moses made a serious mistake during his final days on earth. Rather than speaking to the rock at Meribah—as God had told him—he lost his temper and struck the rock. He not only took credit for himself but did not uphold God's holiness. Consequently, God did not allow him to lead the children of Israel into the Promised Land (see Num. 20:7–13; Deut. 32:31).

An Exception to the Rule

Joshua stands out on the pages of the Old Testament as one of those rare biblical characters who exemplified walking in God's will throughout his entire lifetime. True, he was just as human as his fellow Israelites—and as we are—and at times he made some serious mistakes. But Joshua's mistakes were never as serious as those made by the men who succeeded him.

The reasons for Joshua's persistent and consistent faithfulness to God are vivid in his life story. However, nowhere are those reasons more apparent than in his final words to Israel before he departed this life.

Looking Back

Joshua's final exhortations to God's chosen people involved two historical perspectives following the division of the land among the tribes.

The first perspective was short-range. It included a review of God's faithfulness to Israel in the recent past—that is, since they had crossed over Jordan and experienced victory after victory in the land of Canaan.

The second perspective was long-range. And it included a review of God's faithfulness to Israel since God first chose and called Abraham out of an idolatrous environment in Ur of the Chaldeans and graciously led him and his family into Canaan.

A Great Seven Years

"Joshua was old, advanced in years" as he gathered Israel's leaders together to share with them the burden that lay on his heart (Josh. 23:1). He had completed his earthly task. He had led Israel into the Promised Land. In seven exciting years, they had defeated the Canaanites sufficiently to eliminate any future military threat and resistance.

Joshua had just completed dividing the land among the tribes as God instructed. And now he had some final words about Israel's recent experiences in Canaan:

➤ "You have seen all that the LORD *your God* has done to all these nations because of you" (v. 3a).

- "The LORD *your God* is He who has been fighting for you" (v. 3b).

- "The LORD *your God,* He shall thrust them out from before you and drive them from before you" (v. 5a).

- "You shall possess their land, just as the LORD *your God* promised you" (v. 5b).

- "Cling to the LORD *your God,* as you have done to this day" (v. 8).

- "For the LORD has driven out great and strong nations from before you" (v. 9).

- "The LORD *your God* is He who fights for you" (v. 10).

- "Take diligent heed to yourselves to love the LORD *your God*" (v. 11).

A Serious Warning

Following this series of clear-cut and vivid reminders that it was no one else but the LORD *God of Israel* who had given them the land of Canaan, Joshua made his final point with equal clarity:

"For if you ever go back and cling to the rest of these nations, these which remain among you, and intermarry with them, so that you associate with them and they with you, know with certainty that the LORD *your God* will not continue to drive these nations out from before you; but they shall be a snare and a trap to you, and a whip on your sides and thorns in your eyes, until you perish from off this good land which the LORD *your God* has given you." (vv. 12–13)

"In Conclusion . . ."

Joshua's first historical perspective reminded Israel that it was the *Lord their God* who brought them into the land and gave them victory after victory. It was because of their love for Him and their obedience to His laws that the Lord kept His promises to them. He had been faithful to them because of their faithfulness to Him. But should they forsake the Lord and begin to worship false gods, they would suffer the consequences, losing all they had gained. "'The anger of the LORD will burn against you,'" warned Joshua, "'and you shall perish quickly from off the good land which He has given you'" (v. 16).

The God of Abraham, Isaac, and Jacob

Joshua's second and final address to Israel before he died at age 110 (24:29) was similar in emphasis to his first address. However, it was more comprehensive. Furthermore, it was far more dramatic in terms of the geographical setting.

Between Two Mountains

Joshua once again "gathered all the tribes of Israel to Shechem" (24:1)—a unique and significant place to deliver a farewell message. It was here (at Mount Gerizim and Mount Ebal) that Joshua had previously built an altar to the Lord and had written the laws of God on large tablets of stones and reviewed these laws for all Israel (8:30–35).

Even More Important

It was in this very place that Abraham first received God's promise regarding the fact that He would give Israel the land of Canaan. It was also here Abraham demonstrated his rejection of the false gods by also building an altar to the Lord, the one true God (Gen. 12:6–7).

Even More Dramatic

It was also in this very place that Jacob, on his return from his carnal wanderings in Mesopotamia, cleansed and purified his own household from false gods by burying all his idols and likewise building an altar to the Lord (33:18–20; 35:1–4).

Joshua's primary concern for Israel is crystal clear. He wants them to know that it was the God of Abraham, Isaac, and Jacob who led them to this point in their national history—not only in enabling them to do great exploits in Canaan since they crossed over Jordan, but right from the very beginning when God called Abraham out of Ur of the Chaldeans (Gen. 12:1, 3). Joshua quotes the Lord directly time and time again to make his point:

➤ "I [the Lord your God] took your father Abraham from beyond the River" (Josh. 24:3).

➤ "I sent Moses and Aaron" to Egypt (v. 5).

➤ "I brought your fathers out of Egypt" (v. 6).

➤ "I brought you into the land of the Amorites . . . and I gave them into your hand" (v. 8).

➤ "I delivered you from his [Balaam's] hand" (v. 10).

➤ "I gave them [the Canaanites] into your hand" (v. 11).

➤ "I sent the hornet before you" (v. 12).

➤ "I gave you a land on which you had not labored" (v. 13).

"In Conclusion . . ."

With this rapid series of quotations from the Lord Himself, Joshua again culminated his address with an exhortation to Israel to "fear the LORD and serve Him in sincerity and truth" (v. 14). He warned them to "put away the gods" which their fathers had served "beyond the River and in Egypt" and to "serve the LORD" (v. 14).

"But for Me and My House"

Joshua ended his formal address with what has become known as one of the most powerful and courageous testimonies and witness in all of Scripture. In his old age and perhaps with a quivering voice, he shouted:

"And if it is disagreeable in your sight to serve the Lord, choose for yourselves today whom you will serve: whether the gods which your fathers served which were beyond the River, or the gods of the Amorites in whose land you are living; *but as for me and my house, we will serve the LORD.*" (v. 15)

Becoming God's Man Today

Principles to Live By

In these two culminating messages to Israel lies the basic secret to Joshua's own success as a faithful and committed man of God. His final words reflect his personal philosophy of life as a leader in Israel.

Two foundational principles emerge from these passages and become personal applications for every twentieth-century Christian man and especially for every Christian leader.

Principle 1. We must believe with all our hearts that God is the only true God.

Once Joshua turned from the gods of Egypt, he never forsook the one true God. Twelve times in chapter 23 Joshua referred to the "Lord your God" when reviewing the successes of Israel in the land of Canaan. This demonstrates who was first in his own life. The Lord God of Israel was Joshua's Lord and God.

True Humility

The true test of Joshua's commitment to God is reflected in his humility as he stood that day and addressed Israel. Looking back over the tremendous victories, how easy it would have been to exalt himself. After all, had not God said before they ever crossed Jordan, "This day I will begin to exalt you in the sight of all Israel!" (Josh. 3:7)? Joshua's statement to Israel at that time revealed his true perspective on himself and his relationship to God:

"By this you shall know that the living God is among you, and that He will assuredly dispossess from before you the Canaanite, the Hittite, the Hivite, the Perizzite, the Girgashite, the Amorite, and the Jebusite. . . . [He is] the LORD of all the earth." (vv. 10–11)

The True Test

And now, after God had fulfilled His promises, Joshua was still giving honor and glory to God. True, he realized full well that God had used him as a human instrument to achieve these goals. He did not apologize for the fact that God had used him to cut off these pagan nations and to assign the remaining nations as an inheritance for the tribes of Israel. He did not hesitate to say, "I have apportioned to you these nations" and "I have cut off" all the nations "from the Jordan even to the Great Sea toward the setting of the sun" (23:4). But Joshua also realized full well that it was God who had actually worked on behalf of Israel. Joshua was merely a human instrument utilizing the talents and abilities that God had given him.

A Wonderful Example

This is a great example for every Christian man. It is often easy to begin our Christian life giving glory to God. But as we grow older and as our own accomplishments increase, our natural tendency is to forget the source of our strength, our abilities, our achievements. How easy to exalt and honor ourselves—even to start serving "other gods," particularly the "god of materialism" and the "god of intellectualism."

Like Joshua, we must realize that God uses our talents and our skills. Furthermore, material and intellectual accomplishments are not wrong in themselves. It is not even wrong to use the word "I" to refer to our own efforts. But a Christian who puts God first in his life will always reflect with honesty and true humility that it is God who is responsible for all we are and have. The Christian who has a correct perspective on God's power and grace in his life can only agree with the apostle Paul who, sensing this very thing, wrote with great conviction:

> Now to Him who is able to do exceeding abundantly beyond all that we ask or think, according to the power that works within us, to Him be the glory in the church and in Christ Jesus to all generations forever and ever. Amen. (Eph. 3:20–21)

Principle 2. We must love God with all our hearts.

A Divine Order

It follows naturally that if we truly believe that God is the only true God, we should then love and serve Him. The Lord Himself recognized this divine order when He gave the Ten Commandments. First He said, "You shall have no other gods before Me" (Exod. 20:3), and then He said, I will show "loving-kindness to thousands, to those who love Me and keep My commandments" (v. 6). Joshua followed this order in his own life and urged the children of Israel to do the same.

True Love for God

What does it mean to love God? How is it expressed? These are very important questions, especially for today, since the word "love" is often defined as a purely emotional response. Not so in Scripture.

Joshua answered these questions clearly and specifically in a previous message to the Reubenites, the Gadites, and the half-tribe of Manasseh—the tribes that dwelt beyond the Jordan River. Joshua warned:

> "Only be very careful to observe the commandment and the law which Moses the servant of the Lord commanded you, to love the Lord your God and walk in all His ways and keep His commandments and hold fast to Him and serve Him with all your heart and with all your soul. (Josh. 22:5)

"If You Love Me, You'll Obey Me"

Here indeed is a comprehensive definition of love for God (John 14:21, 24). In short, it means total obedience—doing what God says in every respect and with our total being—our minds, our hearts, our souls. Obviously, our emotions are involved. But obedience often means response to God's will whether we feel like it or not.

Joshua was this kind of man. The overall story of his life reflects obedience to the Lord in everything. And this is why he said unequivocally to Israel in his second farewell address, "'Choose for yourselves today whom you will serve . . . but as for me and my house, *we will serve the LORD.*'" *(Josh. 24:15).*

A Great Model

This statement was the culmination of a life lived in obedience to God's word. At the beginning of Joshua's career as Moses' successor in leading Israel, God said, "'Be strong and very courageous; be careful to do according to all the law which Moses My servant commanded you; do not turn from it to the right or to the left'" (1:7).

And now, years later, Joshua delivered his final words to Israel, in essence the very words God had spoken to him at the beginning of his career: "'Be very firm, then, to keep and do all that is written in the book of the law of Moses, so that you may not turn aside from it to the right hand or to the left'" (23:6).

Faithfulness to God's Commands

There were times, of course, when Joshua failed the Lord—such as when he was deceived by the Gibeonites. There were days when he was discouraged—such as when he failed to trust God following Israel's humiliating defeat at Ai. But the overall direction of his life was obedience.

Joshua's love for God speaks to every Christian man. His life of obedience also illustrates dramatically what Jesus taught His disciples. "'He who has My commandments and keeps them, he it is who loves Me,'" said Jesus. But, "'He who does not love Me does not keep My words'" (John 14:21, 24).

The Greatest Commandment

Jesus emphasized the same thing to a lawyer who one day approached Him and asked a question: "Teacher, which is the great commandment in the Law?" Then Jesus answered: "'You shall love the Lord your God with all your heart, and with all your soul, and with all your mind.' This," said Jesus, "is the great and foremost commandment" (Matt. 22:36–38).

Points of Action

1. To what extent do you really believe that God is the one true God? How is this reflected in your life? True, you may not be bowing down to idols of wood and stone. But what about the gods of materialism and intellectualism? The gods of sensualism? To what extent are you really honoring God above yourself?

2. To what extent do you love God? Is it with your whole heart and soul? What are your areas of disobedience? Do you realize that the degree to which you obey Him is the degree to which you love Him?

Remember!

Love for God is more than feelings. It involves commitment to Him no matter what our emotional response. It involves obedience to Him no matter what our personal desires. Love for God means obeying what He says even though it may hurt. Jesus demonstrated this love when He said in the garden: "'My Father, if it is possible, let this cup pass from Me; yet not as I will, but as Thou wilt'" (Matt. 26:39).

Evaluate!

Check any of the following areas where your life needs the most attention. Pray that God will help you to improve in the areas you check:

___ In your stewardship of time; that is, in the time you give to do His work;

___ In your stewardship of talent; that is, in the way you use your abilities and your skills to serve God;

___ In your stewardship of money; that is, in what you give to help others carry out His work;

___ In your stewardship of prayer; that is, in the time you give to praying about His work.

A Man's Man Is a Godly Man

Reread the questions under Points of Action. Also, review the checklist for evaluating your stewardship of time, talent, money, and prayer. As you do, ask the Holy Spirit to impress on your heart one lesson you need to apply more effectively in your life. Then write out a specific goal. For example, you know that you fall short in your stewardship of prayer. Because of your busy schedule, it's basically crowded out, both in a personal and corporate sense.

Set a Goal

With God's help, I will begin immediately to carry out the following goal in my life:

_____

_____

_____

_____

_____

Memorize the Following Scripture

> *And He said to him, "You shall love the Lord your God with all your heart, and with all your soul, and with all your mind." This is the great and foremost commandment.*
>
> Matthew 22:37–38

Where Should You Go from Here?

*H*opefully, this has been a life-changing study. I know it has if you have done the following:

➤ Studied Joshua's life carefully.

➤ Asked the Holy Spirit to reveal areas in your life that need attention.

➤ Written out goals based on the biblical principles in each chapter.

How Are You Doing?

There's another ongoing step you need to take. Continually evaluate the extent you are reaching the goals you've set.

Following is a summary of the principles from the study of Joshua's life. As you read through these principles, check those where you set a goal. Go back, reread each goal, and ask yourself, "How am I doing?" During this process, isolate those areas to which you need to give more attention.

➤ It takes time to become prepared to be a faithful leader of others.

➤ As Christian men, we must realize there is a unique balance between dependence on God and confidence in ourselves.

> We must begin to serve God now in order to be prepared for future responsibility.

> God wants us to be "strong and courageous"—putting our faith in Him.

> God cares about meeting our needs if we'll just let Him.

> God wants us to take the Word of God and His promises seriously. To do so, we must meditate on the Word and obey what He says.

> Obedience to God's Word brings blessing, now and eternally.

> God will never leave us or forsake us.

> God will forgive our sins if we sincerely turn to Him in repentance and seek His forgiveness.

> God wants us to be responsive to His Word, believing that He has spoken.

> It is God's will that we take a stand against values that are out of harmony with values outlined in Scripture.

> God will honor us if we do not allow a fear of ridicule and persecution to affect our Christian lifestyle.

> God wants us to be active witnesses for Christ, realizing that judgment will come some day.

> God wants us to have a strong faith in Him, even though there are things we do not understand in His great plan for our lives.

> God honors faith, but He does not expect His children to operate on blind faith.

> God honors Christians who honor Him.

> God is still reaching out to lost humanity, and He wants us to be involved in that process.

> God wants us to have "memorial stones" in our homes and in our personal lives that demonstrate that God exists and that we are dependent upon Him for life and existence.

➤ God wants to be a living reality in our lives—not just a theological idea.

➤ God wants us to convey reverence and respect for God to our children.

➤ If you're a Christian, God teaches that you should be baptized in order to demonstrate that you died with Christ and have been resurrected to a new life.

➤ If you're a believer, God wants you to participate regularly in taking Holy Communion. This means you should be an active member of a local church.

➤ God wants all Christians to contribute to the dynamic body life and witness of our church.

➤ God wants each of us to personally share Jesus Christ with non-Christians.

➤ God wants all of us to encourage others to serve in the area of missionary outreach.

➤ God wants all of us financially to support sending others to reach people for Christ.

➤ God wants all of us to pray for those who are serving Jesus Christ in a special way.

➤ God wants all of us to respond to Him as a holy God.

➤ The more light we have, the more we are accountable.

➤ God is displeased with dishonesty.

➤ All who do not know Jesus Christ personally are lost and condemned to eternal judgment.

➤ God will never forsake His children, no matter how much they have forsaken Him.

➤ God can take the mistakes His children make and turn them into positive results.

➤ God gives us freedom to develop a strategic plan, but it must be in harmony with His basic guidelines and principles.

- God wants us to take time out of our busy schedules to review His will for our lives.

- God wants us to develop a priority system that includes regular Bible reading and Bible study.

- God wants us to take advantage of the opportunities He has given us to discover His will for our lives through personal and group Bible study.

- God does not want us to forsake the assembling of ourselves together so that we can develop meaningful relationships with other Christians and with Himself.

- God wants us to pause sufficiently in order to thank Him and praise Him for who He is and what He is going to do for us.

- God wants us to make the Word of God a priority in determining His will for our lives—not our existential experience.

- We can be deceived if we use the Bible "mystically."

- We can be deceived if we read and study the Bible subjectively and without good principles of interpretation.

- We can be deceived if we bring circumstances to bear on Scripture rather than evaluating circumstances in the light of Scripture.

- God honors men who walk in God's will.

- God honors men who take a stand against the majority when the majority are wrong.

- God honors men who take a stand for Him though it means rejection by the group.

- God honors men who faithfully follow Him on the long haul.

- God will never forget men who serve Him faithfully and consistently.

➤ We must believe with all our hearts that God is the only true God.

➤ We must love God with all our hearts.

A Final Challenge

Now that you have reviewed all of the principles we've outlined from a study of Joshua's life and evaluated the way in which you are carrying out the specific goals you've set for your life personally, remember you cannot achieve these goals in your own strength. This is why Paul issued the following exhortations to the Ephesians—and to each one of us:

Finally, be strong in the Lord, and in the strength of His might. Put on the *full armor of God*, that you may be able to stand firm against the schemes of the devil. For our struggle is not against flesh and blood, but against the rulers, against the powers, against the world forces of this darkness, against the spiritual forces of wickedness in the heavenly places. Therefore, take up the full armor or God, that you may be able to resist in the evil day, and having done everything, to stand firm. Stand firm therefore, having girded your loins with *truth*, and having put on the breastplate of *righteousness*, and having shod your feet with the preparation of the *gospel of peace*; in addition to all, taking up the *shield of faith* with which you will be able to extinguish all the flaming missiles of the evil one. And take the *helmet of salvation*, and the *sword of the Spirit*, which is the *word of God*. With all *prayer* and *petition pray at all times in the Spirit*, and with this in view, be on alert with all perseverance and petition for all the saints. (Eph. 6:10–18)

A Final Meditation

I want a principle within of watchful, godly fear,
A sensibility of sin, a pain to feel it near.
Help me the first approach to feel of pride or wrong desire.

To catch the wand'ring of my will,
and quench the kindling fire.
From Thee that I no more may stray, no more Thy goodness
grieve, grant me the filial awe, I pray,
the tender conscience give.
Quick as the apple of an eye,
O God, my conscience make!
Awake my soul when sin is nigh,
and keep it still awake.
Almighty God of truth and love, to me Thy pow'r impart,
The burden from my soul remove,
the hardness from my heart.
O may the least omission
pain my reawakened soul,
and drive me to that grace again,
which makes the wounded whole.[1]

Notes

Introduction

1. Most conservative Christian and Jewish Bible scholars believe that Joshua, the man, was the primary author of Joshua, the book. It is true there are sections he could not have written (such as the record of his death), but there is general agreement that we should credit Joshua with the substantial authorship of the book that bears his name.

Chapter 1

1. These are not just qualities for spiritual leaders in the church. In essence, they are characteristics of maturity for every Christian man. In that sense, they should be spiritual and psychological goals for all of us. For an in-depth study of these qualities, see *The Measure of a Man,* authored by Gene A. Getz and published by Regal Books.

Chapter 3

1. There are some who believe Rahab operated an inn. This is certainly a feasible interpretation. Perhaps she was both a clothmaker and an innkeeper.

Chapter 4

1. For a very helpful summation of these evidences consult Josh McDowell's two volumes—*Evidence That Demands a Verdict and More Evidence That Demands a Verdict* (Arrowhead Springs, Calif.: Campus Crusade for Christ). Both of these books will increase your faith in the reliability of the Scriptures.

Chapter 6

1. For research data, see S.I. McMillen, *None of These Diseases* (Old Tappan, N.J.: Fleming H. Revell Company, 1963), 17–22.

2. Ibid., 20–21.

3. The Passover is designated as the sacrifice, and the feast following the sacrifice is designated as the Feast of Unleavened Bread. These two events are inseparably related and are often simply called the "Passover."

Chapter 7

1. This is not a new phenomenon in the Old Testament. For example, God also appeared to Abraham in human form and conveyed a special message (Gen. 18:1–33).

2. For more detail regarding archaeological discoveries, see Howard F. Vos, *Archaeology in Bible Lands* (Chicago: Moody Press), 179–81. See also Jack Finegan, *Light from the Ancient Past* (London: Oxford University Press), 1:156–59.

Chapter 9

1. At this point, it is difficult to determine how much detail God actually gave Joshua regarding how to carry out this ambush. The text simply records the statement by the Lord to "set an ambush for the city behind it" (Josh. 8:2). The author then moved quickly to a description of the process as Joshua explained his strategy to the people.

It is my personal opinion that the Lord gave these *specific* details to Joshua, and he in turn repeated them to the people. This would be consistent with what the Lord did regarding how to capture Jericho. Furthermore, Joshua needed this kind of security at this time in his life. Specific instructions from the Lord regarding how to capture Ai would certainly contribute to that needed security.

2. Irving L. Jensen gives the following explanation regarding the number of men chosen in Joshua 8:3: "The size of this group is indicated by the text as thirty thousand men, which appears to be an unusually large contingent for such a secret maneuver as ambush close to the city. One plausible answer to the problem is that the text should read 'thirty officers.' This suggestion is made by R.E.D. Clark, who points out that the Hebrew word *elep,* translated 'thousand,' can also be translated as 'chief' or 'officer,' as it is translated in other passages (cf. 1 Chron. 12:23–27; 2 Chron. 13:3, 17; 17:14–19). If this were the case, then the thirty-man group was a highly selected commando unit, assigned to enter the vacated city and burn it.

This view also may better explain the description of the contingent as chosen for being 'mighty men of valor'—more meaningful to a thirty-man group than to a thirty thousand-man unit." Irving L. Jensen, *Joshua Rest—Land Won,* Everyman's Bible Commentary (Chicago: Moody Press, 1966), 72.

3. There are two basic ways to solve the textual problem in this passage. One is to equate the thirty thousand men with the five thousand men who are lying in ambush and explain the numerical discrepancy as a scribal error. This is feasible since these men are described as being located "between Bethel and Ai on the west side of Ai" (Josh. 8:9, 12). The second explanation is that there were two groups of men lying in wait to ambush. The first group was comprised of thirty commandos who were closer to the city (v. 4), backed by a second contingency of five thousand (see note 2 for the explanation regarding

the thirty thousand figure given in v. 3). Personally, I favor the second explanation which is the one I've developed in this chapter.

4. Evidently the king of Ai secured help from the king of Bethel in case of the second attack by Israel. Consequently, those who pursued Israel were from both cities (v. 17).

Chapter 10

1. Why did the author of the Book of Joshua not record the details of Israel's journey from Ai to Mount Ebal? It seems logical to conclude that he wanted to demonstrate dramatically the sharp contrast between the "pile of stones" at the gate of the city and "the altar" at Ebal. To separate these two events with geographical detail would cause the average reader to miss the impact of this contrast, if not lose sight of it altogether.

2. Archaeologists have discovered slabs of stone in this part of the country as long as seven feet. Coating them with lime would create a white base on which Joshua could write very clearly and completely the law of God.

How much of the law was actually written cannot be fully determined from the text of Scripture. It appears, however, that Joshua was very comprehensive, which would be a possibility even in view of the lengthy nature of God's laws in the first five books of Moses. In fact, archaeologists have discovered inscriptions on rocks or stones similar to the process Joshua used. A case in point is one such discovery at Behistun in Iran, which includes information about three times the length of Deuteronomy.

3. From the Joshua record, it is easy to confuse these two sets of stones. A casual reading could lead to the conclusion that the law was written on the altar of stones (Josh. 8:32). A careful reading, however, especially with the background of the more detailed descriptions in Deuteronomy 27, clearly reveals two sets of stones.

4. The representative nature of these statements are reflected in the fact that only twelve are recorded, obviously related to the fact that there were twelve tribes in Israel.

Chapter 12

1. Though numerous battles and victories are recorded in rapid sequence in the Book of Joshua, it should be noted that the process involved a relatively lengthy period of time. It took approximately seven years from the time the children of Israel crossed Jordan and stepped onto the land of Canaan to win sufficient victories to break the military backbone of the Canaanites (11:18, 23).

Conclusion

1. Hymn, "I Want a Principle Written" by Charles Wesley.